Bristol & B

cy(

CU00921166

Rides

Nicky Crowther has asserted her rights to be
identified as the author of this work.

© Nicky Crowther 2004

All rights reserved. No part of this publication may be
reproduced, stored in a retrieval system or transmitted,
in any form or by any means, electronic, mechanical,
photocopying, recording or otherwise, without prior
permission in writing from the publisher.
Published and printed by: Haynes Publishing, Sparkford,
Yeovil, Somerset BA22 7JJ.

British Library Cataloguing-in-Publication Data:
A catalogue record for this book is available
from the British Library.

ISBN 1 84425 025 3

While every effort has been taken to ensure the
accuracy of the information given in this book,
no liability can be accepted by the author or the
publishers for any loss, damage or injury caused by
errors in, or omissions from, the information given.

CONTENTS

Ride location map

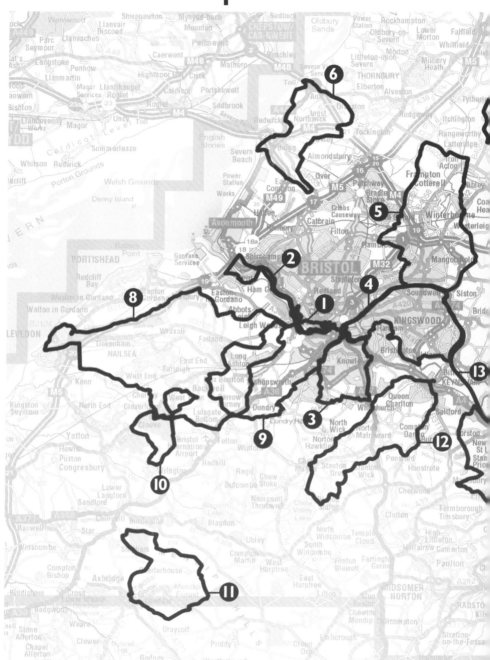

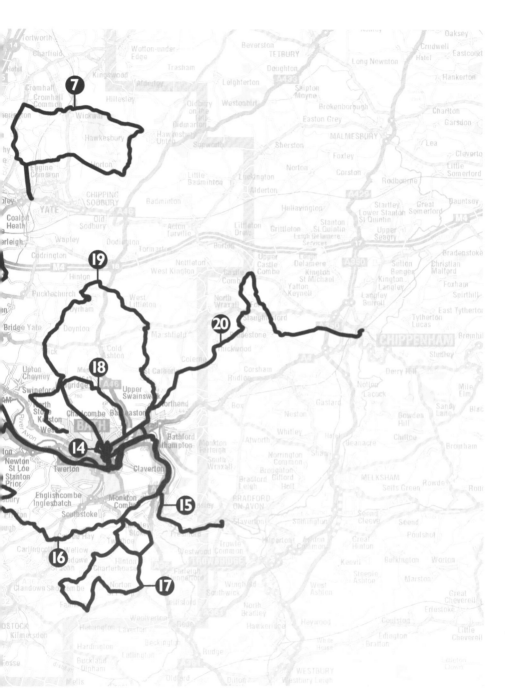

Introduction

ROUTES FOR CHILDREN

Children love to cycle, and cycling is good for children and their parents.

Each route is graded for children according to how flat, long or rough it is. Also, each hazard or tricky road section has been detailed, so please read the assessment and the disclaimer carefully before setting out.

Supervise children carefully. This is particularly important beside water. Tell them to be prepared to dismount quickly when something suddenly comes up, like a low bridge, steep ramp, blind corner or narrow sections. On the road, dismount to turn right, cross busy roads, change lane or make any manoeuvre which puts you in the way of traffic.

Carry snacks to revive little flagging legs and spirits, and don't over-estimate their stamina. Build in rests and offer encouragement. And we wish you many happy adventures together.

Car-free and easy for all ages

2 Avon Gorge (part)
3 Bristol South: Urban bike routes (part)
13 Bristol & Bath Railway Path
15 Kennet & Avon Canal: Bath to Bradford-on-Avon

For stronger, more able children

2 Avon Gorge (in full)
3 Bristol South: Urban bike routes (full)
4 Bristol East: River Avon Towpath and Railway Path
5 Bristol North: Fishponds to Iron Acton
6 Severn Bridges tour
7 Yate to the Cotwold fringes
9 Bristol Southwest MTB: Ashton Court to Dundry
12 Chew Valley lanes: Keynsham to Chew Magna

LITERATURE

Maps

• Ordnance Survey map Landranger 172 1:50,000 (and corresponding Explorer 1:25,000 maps) covers most of the region
• Sustrans NCN Routes 3, 4, 41 (Sustrans

information line tel: 0117 929 0888)
• Bristol Cycling Map (CycleCity Guides, Dome Publishing, 3/4 Zig Zag, Clevedon BS21 7EJ, £4.95)
• Kennet & Avon Canal Navigations map (GeoProjects tel: 0118 939 3567, £4.75) shows the canal in detail from a waterways point of view

Routes book

• Cycle Tours Around Bristol & Bath (23 routes, Philip's, in book shops or Sustrans info line tel: 0117 929 0888, £9)

Route leaflets

• Bristol & Bath Railway Path (Bristol City Council tel: 0117 903 6827), Bath & North East Somerset Council, South Gloucestershire Councils and Avon Valley Partnership, free)
• Cycling in Bath & Beyond (five weatherproof maps, £3.95, availability information from Bath & North East Somerset tel: 01225 395234)
• The Avon Cycleway (a 137km circular road ride around Bristol & Bath, free from Bristol City Council tel: 0117 903 6842)
• Inner Bristol Cycle Map (free from Bristol City Council tel: 0117 903 6842)
• Cycling to Work in North Bristol (free from Bristol City Council tel: 0117 903 6842 and South Gloucestershire Council tel: 01454 863748)
• Malago Greenway (south Bristol, free from Bristol City Council tel: 0117 903 6842)
• Whitchurch Railway Path and St Phillips Greenway (south Bristol, NCN3, free from Bristol City Council tel: 0117 903 6842)
• Cycling in Bradley Stoke (free from South Gloucestershire Council tel: 01454 863748)
• Cycling in Yate (Bristol City Council)

ORGANISATIONS AND CONTACTS

• **Bristol Cycling Campaign**
Contact BCC, c/o Box 60, 82 Colston Street, Bristol BS1 5BB, email@bristolcycling.com, www.bristolcycling.com. Their website features a diary of rides, telephone numbers for problems with cycleways and an online forum.
• **Cycle Bath**
The Bath Cycling Campaign, membership

Hire a bike at Bradford for a lovely day out on the Kennet and Avon Canal (ride 15).

secretary, Angie Whitfield, 82 London Road West, Bath BA1 7DA.

• Sustrans around Bristol & Bath

Bristol is home of the national engineering charity Sustrans (which stands for 'sustainable transport') and works on practical projects to encourage more walking and cycling and to reduce traffic. The National Cycle Network (NCN), the charity's flagship project, passes through urban centres and will eventually reach all corners of the country. Over a third of the total 10,000 miles due for completion in 2005 will be traffic-free.

Bristol and Bath lie on Routes 3 (West Country Way, Bristol to Padstow), 4 and 41 (Severn & Thames, Gloucester to Newbury with a link via Chepstow to the Lon Las Cymru – Welsh National Cycle Route).

Routes in this book that use pieces of NCN include; 2 Avon Gorge, 3 Bristol South Urban, 4 Bristol East, 5 Bristol North, 6 Severn Bridges Tour, 12 Chew Valley, 14 Bristol-Bath

Railway Path, 15 Bath sightseeing, and 16 Bath South lanes. We are therefore most grateful to Sustrans for their foresight and commitment to the cycling cause!

• The CTC – Cyclists' Touring Club

This is the national cyclists' organisation, representing cycling interests and running an excellent information service, also a network of long-established recreational district associations who primarily organise leisure rides (tel: 0870 8730060, website www.ctc.org.uk).

The CTC runs a Bristol District Association and Bath Section. Please contact HQ on the number above.

BIKES ON TRAINS AROUND BRISTOL AND BATH

Trains and bikes go together like a horse and carriage. Let the train take the strain of getting you and your bike to and from the routes. It's one less car.

For times ring National Rail Enquiries on 08457 484950. We've tried to make it clear on each route what the bike carrying conditions are, but for confirmation ring National Rail Enquiries, which can also put you on to the individual train companies (First Great Western tel: 0845 6005604, Wessex Trains tel: 0845 6000880, Wales & Borders tel: 0845 6061660).

CYCLE HIRE (none in Bath)
Bristol
• **Blackboy Cycles** (tel: 0117 973 1420), 180 Whiteladies Road (at the top end, by the clock tower on the edge of the downs)

• **Dundas Aqueduct**
Dundas Enterprises at Brass Knocker Basin/Dundas (eg £14 per day, tel: 01225 722292)

• **Bradford-on-Avon**
Towpath Trail Bikes at the Lock Inn at Bradford (eg £12 per day, tel: 01225 868068)

BIKE SENSE
Security
Ride sensible of risk, for example not alone after dark on towpaths. People have been attacked and their bikes stolen from them on towpaths, with afternoons and evenings the riskier times of day. Don't stop for anyone you consider suspicious who asks the time.

Take a friend for company and security.

Clothing
• Wear loose or cycle clothing that allows freedom of movement.
• If you buy one item of cycling gear, make it first a helmet, close-second, a pair of shorts (you can get baggy ones with inserts inside if you don't fancy figure-revealing lycra). They provide cushioning from the saddle and prevent chafing.
• Wear a top that keeps your shoulders and back fully covered, in case of crashes and to prevent sunburn.
• Always carry waterproofs: cycling in cold, wet clothes will make you miserable.
• Wear sunglasses to protect eyes from dust,

THE OFF-ROAD CYCLING CODE

1 Stay on the trail
Only ride bridleways and byways
Avoid footpaths
Plan your route in advance
Use Explorer/Landranger maps

2 Tell someone where you are going
(and when you expect to be back)
If possible, leave a map of the ride at home

3 Give way to horses
Stop completely for horses – they can take fright and flight
If you do ride past, do it carefully after checking with the rider

4 Give way to walkers
Say 'hello' too!

5 Bunching is harassing
Ride in twos or threes

6 Prevent erosion
Don't skid deliberately

7 Close the gate behind you
(but if it is fastened open, leave it open)
Don't climb walls or force hedges

8 Stay mobile
Wear a helmet
A mobile phone can be a great aid
Carry a First Aid kit
Carry enough food and drink
Pack waterproofs and warm clothes

9 Take pride in your bike
Maintain it before you leave home
Carry essential spares and tools

10 Be tidy
Litter in the countryside is horrible
Guard against fire

11 Keep smiling

River Avon at Crews Hole (ride 4).

insects, trail muck and glare.
• Wear gloves or mitts for better grip and to protect against foliage and falls.

Equipment
• Always wear a helmet. It can prevent or limit brain damage if you hit your head badly. A good fit is essential. The helmet should be snug and move with the scalp if you wiggle your eyebrows, but not tight enough to pinch the sides of your head.
• A helmet that does not fit will not offer adequate protection. A child's head is especially vulnerable, so try to get children and reluctant teenagers into the habit of wearing one from the start.
• A reflective belt and lights are essential should you run out of daylight or if the weather changes. Ankle bands are particularly good for alerting car drivers to your presence. Kit children out in a full set of reflectors.

• In case of emergencies, take small change and a mobile 'phone.
• Always carry a puncture repair kit, spare inner tube and bicycle pump.
• A handlebar computer is a useful aid for seeing how far you have ridden, what your current and maximum speeds are, total and trip mileage, and the time.

Stop Thief!
The majority of bike thefts are opportunist. You leave your machine propped up outside the newsagent and it's gone when you return. So rule number one is always lock it up.

Use a solid steel U-lock (only heavy-duty stranded wire cables are as good) and tie the bike to something immovable like a lamp-post, railings or bike stand. Thread the lock through the frame, the back wheel and the removed front wheel. Take off anything else that unclips; lights, pump, water-bottle, and, if you are really

Pensford village, dominated by the disused railway viaduct (ride 12).

diligent, the saddle.

Insure your bike, either as a named item (if it is worth over a few hundred pounds) on a home contents policy, or individually. Take a photo of it and note the frame number.

Also, have it postcoded at your local police station. Hundreds of recovered bikes a year are never reunited with their owners because police could not trace them.

In case of accident
• Place the rider in the recovery position using the minimum of movement. Keep the rider warm and place a jacket beneth their head for comfort.
• If they have sustained a head injury, do not remove their helmet unless they are bleeding severely.
• Do not give food in case they need to be operated on in a hurry.
• If you have to leave an injured rider to seek assistance, make sure they are warm and feel able to stay awake.
• Make a note of where you have left them on your map and mark the spot with a piece of bright clothing held down by a stone or attached to a tree.
• Get help as quickly as possible.

BIKES ARE LEGAL ON BRIDLEWAYS
Rights of way law forbids cycling on footpaths, but you can ride on bridleways (according to Section 30 1968 Countryside Act).

CYCLING ON THE CANALS
The Kennet & Avon Canal towpath, which we follow inland upstream from the River Avon in Bath, is part of the National Cycle Network and therefore upgraded and in fine condition. Nonetheless, you must give way to other users and always cycle considerately. The guidelines below apply to all towpaths.

Below: The Ring O' Bells at Priston (ride 16).

THE WATERWAYS CODE

British Waterways does its best to keep the waterways in good repair. As more and more people discover the charm and tranquility of the waterways, there are increased risks of conflict and damage to the environment. So please follow the advice below and enjoy your visit to the waterway safely.

Permits

• You need a permit to cycle on towpaths, and information telling you which stretches are open to cyclists (all the sections on these routes are). Permits are free and available with an information pack from British Waterways Customer Services, Willow Grange Church Road, Watford WD17 4QA (tel: 01923 201120, enquiries.hq@britishwaterways.co.uk, www.britishwaterways.co.uk).

Look after your waterways

• Avoid cycling where your tyres would damage the path or verges (eg when they are wet or soft).

Consider others

• Give way to others on the towpath and warn them of your approach. Pedestrians have priority. A polite 'hello' and 'thank you' mean a lot.
• Watch out for anglers' tackle and give them time to move it before you try to pass.
• Dismount under low, narrow or blind bridges.
• Never race one another or perform speed trials.
• We recommend you obtain third party liability insurance and equip your bike with a bell or equivalent.

Take care

• Please dismount alongside locks.
• Access paths can be steep and slippery – join and leave the towpath with care.
• You must get off and push your cycle beneath low or blind bridges, and where the path is very narrow.
• We strongly advise against cycling on the towpath after dark, but if you have to, use front and rear lights.
• Thorny hedge trimmings can cause punctures – plastic-reinforced tyres are recommended.

Surviving the traffic

Don't let heavy traffic put you off riding around a city. With assertiveness, awareness and a tad of fitness, you can claim your space on the tarmac and enjoy being in control of your journey.

There are bad and careless drivers and good cyclists. The reverse is also true. Safety depends on two factors: awareness of potential hazards and how to avoid them; and considerate cycling techniques designed to catch the attention of other drivers and help them to help you.

Cycling hazards

Left-hand bends
Indicate to request space as you swing round a left-hand bend so you don't get squeezed. Cars tend not to allow for your travel space. Indicate with your right arm.

Gaps in your line of traffic
This can mean space is being left for a car outside your vision to turn into. Brake and approach with great care.

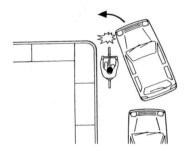

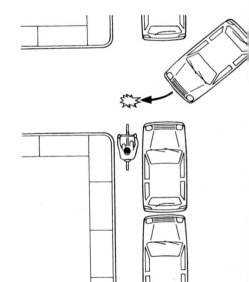

Drafting
Drafting or slipstreaming vehicles is fast, furious fun, so naturally, it is dangerous. Vehicles brake more quickly than bikes, especially in the wet.

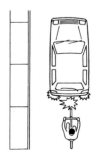

Bollards
These help pedestrians, but hinder cyclists. Anticipate that you may be squeezed, and request space by sticking out an arm in good time.

Car doors opening

Leave 1 metre between you and any parked cars. Catch the driver's eye in their wing mirror.

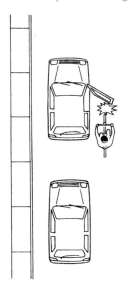

Being crushed by lorries or buses

Never get on the inside of buses, coaches or lorries going left. The most frequent cause of cycling fatalities is a rider being crushed as the vehicle cuts off the apex of the corner. At lights wait behind big vehicles, and let them go ahead around corners.

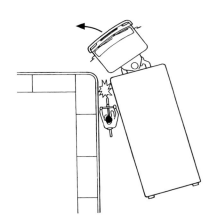

GOOD CYCLING TECHNIQUES

Indicate and communicate
Use big arm movements in plenty of time to let drivers react. Make eye contact. Call out. Use a bell. Thank a helpful manoeuvre with a thumbs-up or the like.

Be well lit at night
Drivers see only lights after dark, not shadows. Reflective strips are a great aid.

Be patient and control your temper
Learning to handle the occasional idiot is part of becoming a true cyclist.

Don't be late
Cycling takes skill, nerve and balance. If you are worried or late, you are putting yourself at risk. Keep your mind on the riding.

Get reasonably fit
Then you can flow with the traffic, not against it, get out of small spaces quicker – and enjoy yourself more.

Bristol Sightseeing

A cycle-friendly tour with a wealth of sights including the fascinating harbour, Clifton Suspension Bridge and townscape, the Cabot Tower, St Mary Redcliffe and elegant Queen's Square.

What to see
The Industrial Museum
(Tel: 0117 925 1470; admission free; open Apr-Oct 10am-5pm Sat-Weds, closed Thurs-Fri; the rest of the year 10am-5pm Sats-Suns only.)

This museum occupies the dockside beside Princestreet Bridge where railway wagons, ships and cranes stand on the quayside and go into action on many weekends throughout the year. Inside are about 400 exhibits from road and rail, plus Bristol-made aero engines and other aviation artefacts including a Concorde cockpit.

The Floating Harbour and Docks
Lining both banks of the former docks is a fascinating mixture of historic and modern buildings at the heart of the city's action. Here is the trendy bike shop and cafe Mud Dock, the Arnolfini and Watershed arts centres, Millennium Square (with summertime designer play fountains) and @Bristol.

RIDE INFORMATION

Distance 10km (6 miles)
Car-free 4km (2.5 miles) (42%)

Grade
Easy-moderate; there is a 500m long climb up Bridge Valley Road to Clifton, which some folks will walk, but it is not terribly onerous (Clifton is worth the effort). Coming down off Brandon Hill, Brandon Steep is as it says and unless you are very confident of your brakes, you may wish to walk down this road. Here and there are other little rises and drops. Also, on the harbourside watch for: railway lines and even trains running on some days; cables and bollards; also give way to people on foot.

Suitability for children and occasional riders?
See Grade. You could also quite happily stick to the car-free harbourside between the Arnolfini and the start of the Avon Gorge (4km return)

Traffic
What traffic there is is light, or we use pavement cycle routes. There is one right-turn on to Park Street near College Green which needs care

Start/finish
The Arnolfini arts centre (Narrow Quay) on the waterfront (with a spur to Bristol Temple Meads station for anyone coming in by train)

Stations
Bristol Temple Meads, Clifton Down (1km east of route in Clifton), Bedminster (1km south of route at Redcliffe)

Bristol is home to Sustrans, creator of the National Cycle Network.

Sunshine after showers in the modernistic city centre.

Refreshments
Mud Dock Cafe (tel: 0117 934 9734, 40 The Grove, near the Arnolfini); the Arnolfini and the Watershed (the waterfront); the Dock Cafe (quayside near *SS Great Britain*); the Cottage pub quayside near the end of the harbour; cafes in Sion Hill, Clifton

Literature
Bristol TIC has further details on the sights; the *Inner Bristol Cycle Map* shows more cycle lanes (free, tel: city council 0117 903 6827)

Bike shops
Dave Bater Cycles at the bottom of Park Street (tel: 0117 929 7368); Mud Dock Cycleworks (tel: 0117 929 2151) near the Arnolfini; Blackboy Cycles, 180 Whiteladies Road (at the top end, by the clock tower on the edge of the downs, tel: 0117 973 1420)

(tel: 0845 345 1235), a contemporary science museum, excellent for children, with dozens of interactive exhibits (Explore), a tropical wildlife and planthouse (Wildwalk), Planetarium and Imax cinema.

SS Great Britain
Designed in 1843 by Isambard Kingdom Brunel, the first ocean-going iron ship driven by a screw propeller made dozens of trips to Australia in the age of the sailing ship. Badly damaged rounding Cape Horn in 1886

Find the Bristol Industrial Museum on the Floating Harbour near the start of the route.

however, it was deemed too expensive to repair and languished in the Falkland Islands being used as nothing more than a beached warehouse. Enthusiasts couldn't let such a historic vessel rot, and in 1970 she was carefully towed back to Bristol and is undergoing continuing reconstruction in dry dock (tel: 0117 926 0680; open daily 10am–5pm (to 4.30pm in winter); admission £6/4 adult/child).

Clifton Suspension Bridge
Isambard Kingdom Brunel's first ever commission was actually only completed five years after his death in 1864. It soars 75m above the gorge connecting Clifton and Leigh Woods, a monument to the great engineer and a beautiful structure that caps Clifton's charm (pedestrians and cyclists cross free, cars 20p). A dedicated visitor centre (tel: 0117 974 4664) is located in a nearby Georgian house.

Nearby, an observatory houses a camera obscura and has great views of the bridge.

Bristol Cathedral
Founded in 1140 as the church of an Augustinian monastery, on College Green, it became a cathedral in 1542. It has a striking Norman Chapter house and a 14th century choir although much of the nave and western towers were constructed as late as 1868.

St Mary Redcliffe
Judged of greater architectural interest than the cathedral, the church of St Mary Redcliffe is a prime example of English perpendicular, with a grand hexagonal porch.

Brandon Hill Park and the Cabot Tower
The best views in Bristol are from the top of the Cabot Tower (climb up a spiral stone

Above: The harbourside Arnolfini arts centre, left, is the start of the route. Below: Georgian elegance in Queen's Square

RIDE

I

The view from Redcliffe Bridge shows a thriving river life.

The Cabot Tower, Brandon Hill, has wonderful views across the city.

staircase; closes at dusk), built to commemorate John Cabot's voyage in the ship *Matthew* from Bristol to discover Newfoundland in 1497. The tower lies in Brandon Hill Nature Park.

Tourist office

Bristol TIC (tel: 0906 586 2313, email: ticharbourside@bristol-city.gov.uk, website: www.VisitBristol.co.uk) is at the @Bristol complex at Harbourside in the centre.

There is so much distraction on this route, it is doubtful anyone will ever complete it in one go. There's your challenge!

Starting from the harbourside at the Arnolfini Art Gallery, we ride along the Floating Harbour (the former docks) past all manner of old and new structures, the SS *Great Britain* and a replica of Cabot's *Matthew*, all with fine views up to Clifton, as far as the great brick Wills warehouses where the harbour meets the tidal River Avon.

From there we ride on pavement cycle lanes from the Avon Gorge up to Clifton (you may be walking for a minute or two), to visit the magnificent suspension bridge and feast on splendid Georgian architecture, including Royal York Crescent (stop and hop up on to the terrace).

Heading back to the city centre, we drop sharply via a stretch on foot through Brandon Hill Nature Park (the Cabot Tower), to emerge at the bottom of Park Street in front of Bristol Cathedral and the fine curving Council House. Back at the waterfront we cross Millennium Square with its modernist fountains, pass along the waterfront by the Watershed arts centre to visit cobbled King Street, the centre of old Bristol, St Mary Redcliffe church and return via Queen's Square to the waterfront.

A spur leads from St Mary Redcliffe to Temple Meads station.

Please walk the bike through Brandon Hill Nature Park as no cycling is allowed, and it is the nicest way to cross the park. Watch right-hand turns near Cumberland Basin and on to Park Street.

RIDE
I

Link from Temple Meads station

At the station exit on the main road, go right and get into the central segregated bike lane, follow 100m as far as the old hotel and go left between the hotels. Cross at the pedestrian/cycle crossing slightly to the left, heading towards St Mary Redcliffe and go straight ahead on the side street, Portwall Lane. Continue on this as far as St Mary Redcliffe, then pick up the route.

1 *Start at the Arnolfini arts centre, on the harbour corner opposite the Watershed. Head south across the little road swingbridge, Princestreet Bridge, and go right along the quayside in front of the Industrial Museum (watch out for the railway lines which are stll used by steam trains on some days.) and continue beside the water for 1km to the SS Great Britain. Turn inland here and after just 150m or so, at the far end of the old brick building, go right on a footpath and emerge near new housing. Turn right again back to the water, and continue round the marina along the harbour for another 500m as far as the Cottage pub. Go left here to main Cumberland Road, and right along the pavement for 300m. Turn right down Avon Crescent, and at the end, go left on the slip road in front of the brick cottages and up to the traffic lights, and then right, down to the front of the great brick Will's warehouse (now the Create Centre). Go right under the flyover, and cross carefully immediately opposite the road bridge over the footbridge, then the lock gates to reach the far side of the harbour (Cumberland Basin, where it meets the Avon river).*

2 *Reach the pavement of the A4 Hotwell Road and go left heading into the Avon Gorge beneath the suspension bridge (cycling on the pavement). After 1km, turn right at the lights up Bridge Valley Road (cycle-signed for Clifton) and walk or ride to the top. At the junction, go right into Clifton Down, signed for the bridge and after 1km (passing grand houses) right again across the green to Suspension Bridge Road where another right leads to the bridge (views from the middle). The observatory is up to the right, and the visitor centre is down the hill.*

3 *Go down the path to the road below, and right (Sion Hill) towards the Avon Gorge*

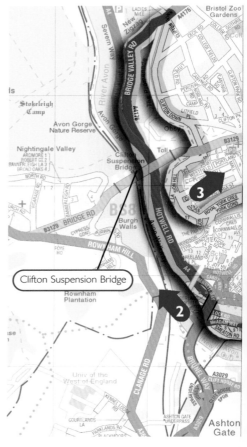

Clifton Suspension Bridge

Hotel. Continue, curving round left, and after 300m turn left into Royal York Crescent. (The terrace is best viewed from the pavement above.) At the end, head right, into Regent Street and continue for 400m past Goldney Hall (on right). Go right steeply down Constitution Hill (ride carefully) and at the end, cross with care over Jacobs Wells Road, and mount the steps directly ahead, into Brandon Hill Nature Park.

4 *Walk across the park (Cabot Tower is up to the left with the best views from the top), and down to the far right-hand corner (although ahead is Great George Street, location of the preserved Georgian House (tel: 0117 921 1362, No. 7). Emerge with care left, down the*

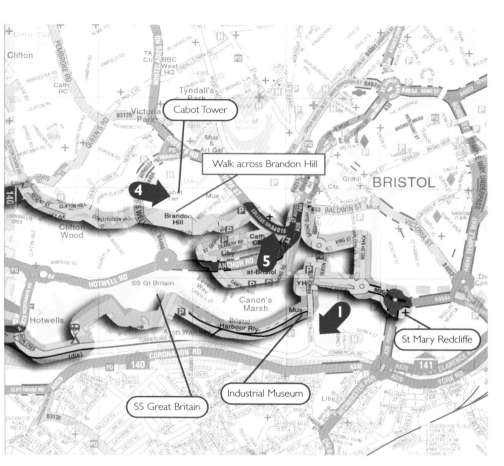

Cabot Tower

Walk across Brandon Hill

BRISTOL

SS Great Britain

Industrial Museum

St Mary Redcliffe

very sharp Brandon Steep – walking might be a good option for some. At the mini-roundabout at the bottom, go left up short St George's Road to Park Street at the top. (The Wills Building, part of the university, is at the top of the street). Go carefully right, and in front of the Council House and cathedral, cross the road at the cycle lights.

Head straight over the green to the cathedral, bear right and continue parallel to the buildings into the roadway (College Green/ Deanery Road). A little way along, turn left sharply down Partition Street to the main road (Anchor Road). Go straight ahead into Canon's Way. At the end you will find Millennium Square and the @Bristol centre (Explore, Wildwalk and Imax cinema).

5 Follow pavement cycle signs left through the square, towards the harbourside. Follow signs left again behind the Watershed media centre and bars, to the end of the short harbour arm. Go right and carefully join the bus way to the small planted roundabout, then first left down cobbled King Street. Continue to the end at the waterside.

Turn right (Welsh Back) and left over Redcliffe Bridge, to St Mary Redcliffe on the right (for Temple Meads station continue for 500m). Turn around, recross Redcliffe Bridge and go straight ahead along one side of Queen's Square, and then straight over the road at the end to Pero's bridge. The Arnolfini is to your left.

21

The Avon Gorge, City Centre to Avonmouth

Bristol's most spectacular ride has views of vertiginous cliffs from tranquil riverbanks. Travel through the gorge right from the city centre almost to the sea and back, using both sides of the River Avon.

Here's a unique Bristol ride of towering cliffs, quaint creeks and peaceful river scenes, nearly all on pleasant cycle routing.

From the harbourside in central Bristol (assuming you can tear yourself away from that) enter the Avon Gorge beneath Clifton Suspension Bridge and head out along the west bank of the river on a simple dirt towpath (rougher in places) for 7km as far as

RIDE INFORMATION

Distance	23.5km (15 miles)
Car-free	21km (13.5 miles) (89%)
Grade	Easy (flat throughout, with short rises)

Suitability for children and occasional riders?
Very suitable, just out on the west bank towpath through the gorge and back, although the full return circuit will be beyond young children and involves more difficult parts

Traffic
21km of car-free riding follows the riverside towpath (NCN4) out through the gorge, and the pavement-shared cycle path back, with short pieces of roadway through Pill village (800m) and Shirehampton (1.5km), and one crossing of the dual carriageway Portway A4 on foot

Start/finish
The Arnolfini beside Princestreet swing bridge on the harbour near the Industrial Museum

Stations
Bristol Temple Meads, Sea Mills, Shirehampton (both on the Severn Beach line from Temple Meads)

Refreshments
Mud Dock Cafe, the Arnolfini, the Dock Cafe (near *SS Great Britain*), waterfront pub in Pill

Literature
This lies partly on NCN4/41, full maps from Sustrans

Bike shops
Dave Bater Cycles at the bottom of Park Street (tel: 0117 929 7368)

Mud Dock Cycleworks (tel: 0117 929 2151) near the Arnolfini

What to see
The Floating Harbour, *SS Great Britain* and Clifton Suspension Bridge (see Bristol Sightseeing)

Entering the gorge beneath the
Clifton Suspension Bridge.

the creekside hamlet of Pill. Then comes the cycle path that leads over the M5 motorway bridge, and acts as a turnaround point. A short stretch leads back through the streets of Shirehampton to reach the pavement-shared cycle path on the main A4 road that draws you spectacularly back through the gorge. We return through the city beside the New Cut of the river as far as Bathurst Basin near the Arnolfini (with a link to Temple Meads station).

From the old Wills's warehouses to the M5 motorway bridge, we follow NCN4, which is signed in most places.

The only traffic issues come crossing a few roads, making the right turn in the middle of Shirehampton, and crossing the A4 Portway dual carriageway. The motorway bridge cycle path is naturally completely segregated.

Enjoy the Avon Gorge on both sides of the river, on designated cycle paths.

1 Start at the Arnolfini art centre, on the harbour corner opposite the Watershed. Go south across the little road swingbridge, Princestreet Bridge, and go right on the quayside in front of the Industrial Museum (watch out for the railway lines and trains) and continue beside the water for 1km to the SS Great Britain. Turn inland here, and after just 150m or so, at the far end of the old brick building, go right on a footpath and emerge near new housing. Turn right again back to the water, and continue round the marina along the harbour for another 500m as far as the Cottage pub. Go left here and at the main Cumberland Road turn right and continue for 300m to opposite Avon Crescent.

2 Cross Cumerland Road with care, go through the railings and right, westward, on to the path along the river New Cut, NCN4 (which we follow to the M5 motorway bridge).

Continue to the warehouses, and, following NCN4 signs turn left over the disused railway bridge, right at the end and follow the tarmac path beneath the flyover to pick up the west bank Avon towpath through the gorge beneath the Clifton Suspension Bridge.

3 Head for 6km to where the path turns inland at pretty Chapel Pill. Continue with NCN4 signs onto open space at Pill, and at a path junction with a grassy mound ahead and right, go straight ahead then right, keeping the mound on your right, continuing down to the viaduct. Joining the road, go beneath the viaduct and right on Underbanks continuing beside the water on Marine Parade, then right on Avon Road and left after 150m up to the cycle track beside the railway line. Follow that to the ramp up the M5 motorway bridge cycle path, and cross the bridge over the river.

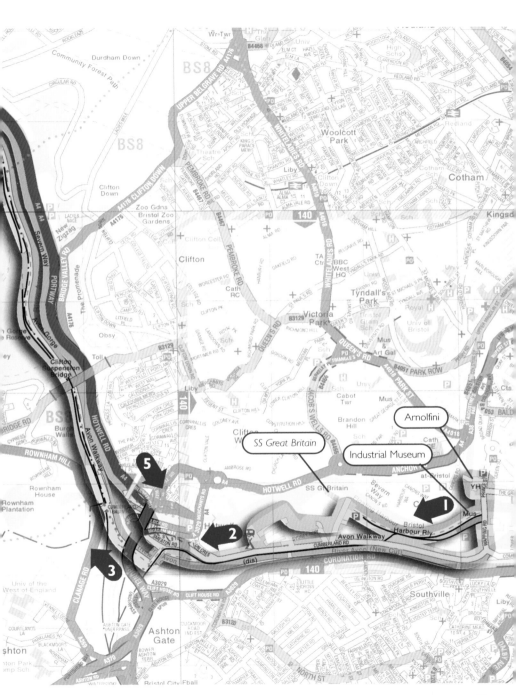

SS Great Britain

Arnolfini

Industrial Museum

25

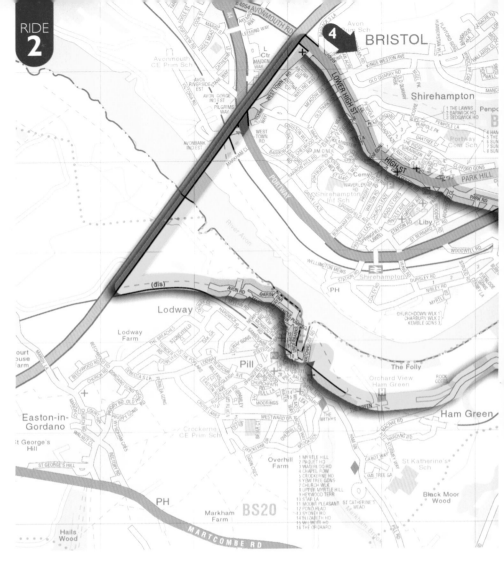

4 Coming off the bridge in Shirehampton, at the road turn right and continue (here we leave NCN4) for 1km up through the middle of town (Lower High Street/High Street). At the green, go right carefully down Park Road, and at Portway A4 dual carriageway at the bottom, cross with great care to the far pavement (shared cycle path), and then left, heading back upriver through the gorge towards Bristol.

Continue for 5km on the shared cycle path back as far as the lock where the Bristol floating harbour meets the river.

5 Cross at the lock gates, then the footbridge that brings you out on the road near the old Will's warehouse, now the Create Centre. Make your way under the flyovers to the warehouse front, and retrace your steps back along the bike path, presently running back along the river New Cut. Proceed for 1.5km, following the path up on to the pavement (shared) of Cumberland Road, as far as the left-hand turn-off, Wapping Road, at Bathurst Basin, that leads back over the swingbridge to the Arnolfini.

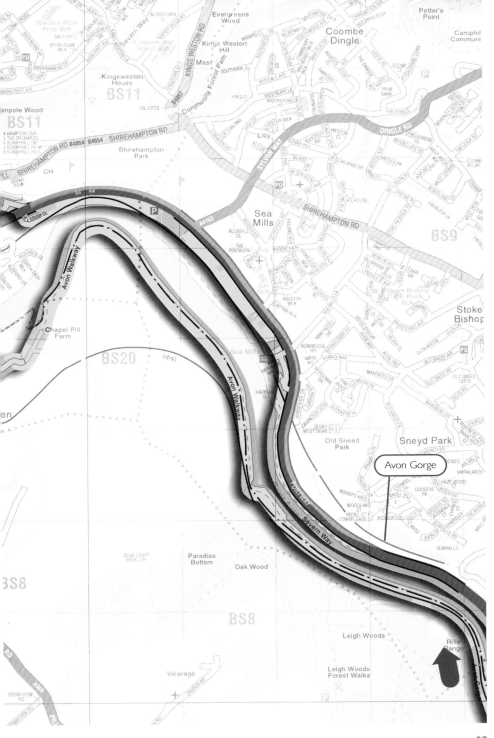

Bristol South: urban bike routes

Explore Bristol's southern nooks from the River Avon as far up as Hartcliffe and back on a patchy circuit linking three cycle paths

This is not a route of beauty – it is fragmented and runs through mostly plain suburbs – but it might satisfy people who live nearby or who like to discover nooks of car-free riding in the city. The nicest sections run through Victoria Park (Windmill Hill), up the wooded climb (the most rural feeling of the lot) at Crox Bottom below Hartcliffe and beside the Avon river.

Car-free cycle paths have been installed in four places. We travel away from the centre from Bedminster on the Malago Greenway beside the Malago stream using riverside paths and open spaces, then do a broken climb to Willmotte Park in Hartcliffe. We bridge an anonymous 3km eastward to reach the Whitchurch Railway Path, for a smooth downhill 2km run back to the centre, and, after 2km further bridging on roads, join the fine St Philip's Greenway along the north bank of the Avon for 2km back to Temple Meads.

There are few hazards, apart from the steady climb to the top of the route in Hartcliffe, the annoyance that dumping is prevalent in the poor little Malago, and that the old railway has been built over.

The Whitchurch Railway Path is on NCN3, which continues on roads south to Chew Magna (see Route 12, the Chew Valley).

RIDE INFORMATION

Distance 14.5km (9 miles)
Car-free 1.5km (1 mile) (11%)
Grade Moderate, with some rough paths and a long steady climb to the city limits

Suitability for children and occasional riders?
Only in disconnected parts. There are too many roads and the overall climb is too great. But you can enjoy the three sections of car-free cycle path: in Victoria Park (Windmill Hill), the Whitchurch Railway Path and the St Philip's Greenway along the Avon riverbank

Start/finish
Bristol Temple Meads station, or anywhere

on what is a circular route (you can ride clockwise or anticlockwise)

Stations
Bristol Temple Meads, Bedminster

Refreshments
Nowhere of note en route, although the cafe at Windmill Hill City Farm (150m off route from Victoria Park, Windmill Hill) serves hot food and there is bike parking

Bike shops
Dave Bater Cycles at the bottom of Park Street (tel: 0117 929 7368)

Mud Dock Cycleworks (tel: 0117 929 2151) near the Arnolfini

Winter sunlight filters through the trees at Windmill
Hill in Bedminster, en route for the southern suburbs.

1 *Starting from Temple Meads station, go left on the pavement at the bottom of the forecourt along the main road to the traffic lights (Cattle Market Road). Continue straight over, and across the river bridge. At the start of the busy two-lane road uphill (Bath Road), cross with care at the lights, and ride on the far side, next to the showroom, take the little barriered road, Mead St (perpendicular to the Bath Road, between the industrial units). Proceed to the end, and go left into the busier St Luke's Road. Beyond the railway bridge, go right into Windmill Hill Park. Cycle uphill, keeping parallel with the railway line, and continue 500m past the school towards colourful houses to where a road crosses (Windmill Hill Close) and goes beneath the railway lines at Bedminster station.*

Follow signs for the Malago Greenway, continuing on the cycle path parallel to the railway line. Stay with that for another 400m to the next major road crossing at Bedminster Road/St John's Lane. Cross this junction and stay with the Malago Greenway into parkland beside the stream. Continue 600m to the end, which is an unsigned road T-junction at an industrial estate with Nover Hill to the left.

2 *Here, go right, and first left into Hastings Road. At the busy road at the end, Hartcliffe Way, go left and ride on the shared pavement-cycle path for 1.2km (leave the Malago Greenway which heads off right). Continue, rising, and watch for the entrance to a green pathway on the right. Cross Hartcliffe Road with care, and follow a streamside path upwards to Crox Bottom. Climb through woods for 600m (including some steep sections) all the way, to the end at the top.*

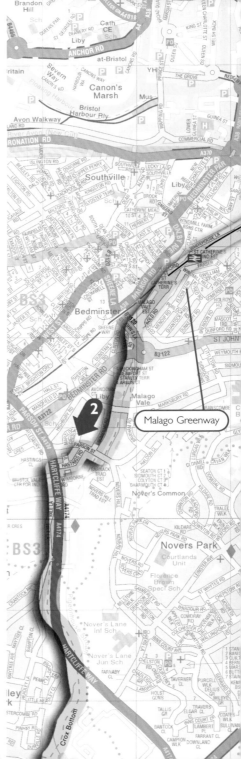

St Philip's Greenway

Whitchurch Railway Path

RIDE
3

3 Fork left at the top of the woods and head towards the main road, Hengrove Way. Bear left on the sliproad then right through the subway beneath the road. This is the start of Willmotte Park, a grassy open space that climbs virtually to the foot of the hills. Cycle route surfacing work is planned for its full length of 1km (but until this is in place, on the first section, go right and take the first left, Stillingfleet Road, up to the end). At Fulford Road, turn left and then right on the grassland path uphill. At Hareclive Road, go right and then left uphill. At the top, Bishport Avenue marks the end of Willmotte Park.

4 Now ride roads eastward 3.5km to pick up the Whitchurch Railway Path and then turn back to the centre. Turn left and continue for 1km as far as a left-hand bend, to go right steeply into Lampton Avenue. Take the second left, Totshill Drive and continue to the end. Go left into Longway Avenue and at the T-junction at the end, Whitchurch Lane, go right carefully. Continue for 1.1km, to a left-hand bend with a country lane on the right. Turn right on to that, Washing Pound Lane, and on through fields.

At the end, go left into Church Road and continue to the traffic lights (Bristol Road). Go straight over at Staunton Lane and after 200m follow signs left for NCN3 (north) on to the Whitchurch Railway Path.

5 Stay on the signed Whitchurch Railway Path for 2km. Leave at the end, via Manston Close and go left on the main road, Sturminster Road. At the roundabout (West Town Lane), cross carefully and continue in the same direction through the new housing estate (not left or right on West Town Lane). At the end, take the subway beneath the embanked road and continue (not left under another subway) bearing on a narrow track (right of Tesco). At the end, emerge at Water Lane.

6 At Water Lane go left, continue 250m to the one-way system. Turn left and then left again into Talbot Road.

At the bridge (which is one-way only, in the opposite direction) dismount and walk across

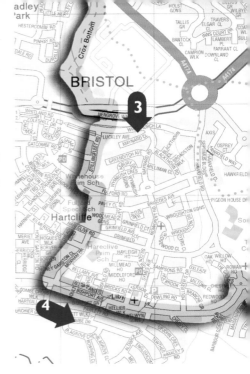

with care. Take the second right, Hampstead Road, and continue to the end (straight over Kensington Park Road), the wall of Arno's Grove Park. Go right, and enter the park left. Follow the bike path right, to the bottom right-hand corner of the park and exit.

Cross straight over the main Bath Road at the pedestrian lights, and take the little road heading in more or less the same direction, Bloomfield Road. Follow this and cycle-signing, joining the right-hand pavement to the roundabout. Stay on the right pavement anticlockwise round the roundabout and continue over the River Avon.

7 On the far side of the bridge, go right down the ramp to join the riverside path below, St Philip's Greenway. Turn right beneath the bridge (the river on your left) and continue beside the river 1km to the end near Temple Meads station.

At the road, Feeder Road/Cattle Market Road, go left signed to Temple Meads — you can use the right-hand pavement. Continue beneath the long railway bridge to the big road junction. Temple Meads station is on your right.

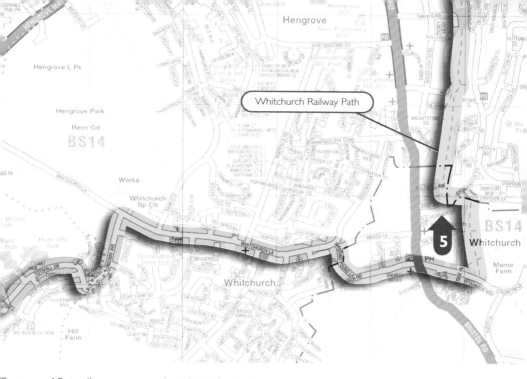

Whitchurch Railway Path

See one of Bristol's attractive multi-coloured terraces from Windmill Hill Park, near the start of the route.

Bristol East: River Avon Towpath and Railway Path

Enjoy a largely car-free circuit from the city centre out along the scenic River Avon, returning on the Bristol & Bath Railway Path.

Car-free riding, refreshments with character at Hanham Lock and Bitton station and a very scenic stretch along the River Avon make this a satisfying tour that hardly leaves the city. But after wet weather, only a sturdy bike with fat tyres will get down the riverside bridleway between Conham and Hanham.

The opening 12km along the River Avon is the route's scenic highlight, where the river undercuts Totterdown and slides past Crew's

RIDE INFORMATION

Distance	28km (17.5 miles)
Car-free	18km (11 miles) (63%)
Grade	Moderate (the riverside path is rough and very muddy in wet/flood conditions)

Suitability for children and occasional riders?
In dry conditions, yes, as long as they can handle the distance, in wet, no. The riverside section is too rough. The Railway Path is always good (see Route 3)

Traffic
At Netham 1km busy road section including a filter right turn; for 2.5km after Hanham past Willsbridge

Start/finish
Bristol Temple Meads station (or anywhere en route)

Station   Bristol Temple Meads

Literature
The Bristol & Bath Railway Path leaflet

(Bristol City Council tel: 0117 903 6827); Sustrans map/route *NCN4* (tel: 0117 929 0888); *Avon Cycleway* leaflet (137km circular road)

Refreshments
Pubs at Hanham Lock, the Old Lock & Weir and Chequers; Bitton station cafe (eat in an old carriage); seasonal kiosk at Old Warmley station (Railway Path)

Bike shops
Dave Bater Cycles at the bottom of Park Street (tel: 0117 929 7368)

Mud Dock Cycleworks (tel: 0117 929 2151) near the Arnolfini

What to see
Bitton station, home of the Avon Valley Railway, restored vintage trains steam up regularly (general enquiries tel: 0117 932 5538, 24-hour talking timetable tel: 0117 932 7296); Railway Path features (see Route 3)

Hole to Conham. The unsurfaced bridleway on to Hanham is the prettiest part but changes dramatically with the seasons. The river has been known to rise and cover the path, which is eroded. When we went, the Old Lock & Weir pub at Hanham Lock was closed due to flooding.

What a disappointment, as this and its sister pub, the Chequers, occupy a lovely site at Hanham Lock, and make the most of it with outside tables. The buffet at Bitton station at the start of the railway path section is another charming, albeit beer-free, place to refuel.

The railway path is an efficient way back to the city centre, if straight in places. In good

weather, when the ground is firm, you could simply retrace your steps from Hanham Lock back along the river to repeat the scenic satisfaction.

Willsbridge Mill, on the road link between Hanham and Bitton station, belongs to the Avon Wildlife Trust, with an old brick mill and nature reserve in the wooded valley of Siston Brook. Meanwhile, vintage trains run from the Avon Valley Railway's Bitton station.

Moves are afoot to allow cycling along the riverside path, the Avon Walkway, directly at Netham Lock all the way to Conham. At the time of research cyclists still had to follow the pleasant riverside lane on this stretch.

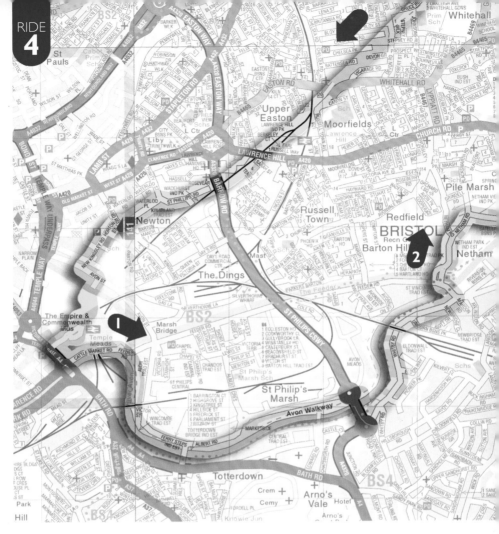

① From Temple Meads station forecourt go left on the pavement, and after 150m at the traffic lights go left again, on the pavement cycle path, into Cattle Market Road, beneath the railway bridge. Beyond the bridge turn right on St Philip's Greenway riverside cycle path, and continue for 2km to the end. Beyond the road bridge, take the ramp that leaves the riverside up to the left. At the top, take the cycle path left to cross the bridge to the roundabout.

② At the roundabout, go left into Whitby Road, signed for St Anne's. Continue for 1km to the T-junction with Feeder Road and Netham Lock. Go left, cross the river and Netham Lock, then, carefully, immediately filter right (lane change) into busy Netham Road. (In the future it is hoped that cyclists will be allowed to join the Avon riverside path at this point.)

③ Climb, then after 500m go right carefully down Crew's Hole Road (signed Crew's Hole) to regain the riverside riding on the road. Continue for 1.8km to the wooded point (Conham) where the river bends right away from the road. There join the unsurfaced bridleway towing path. Continue for 4km as far as Hanham Mills.

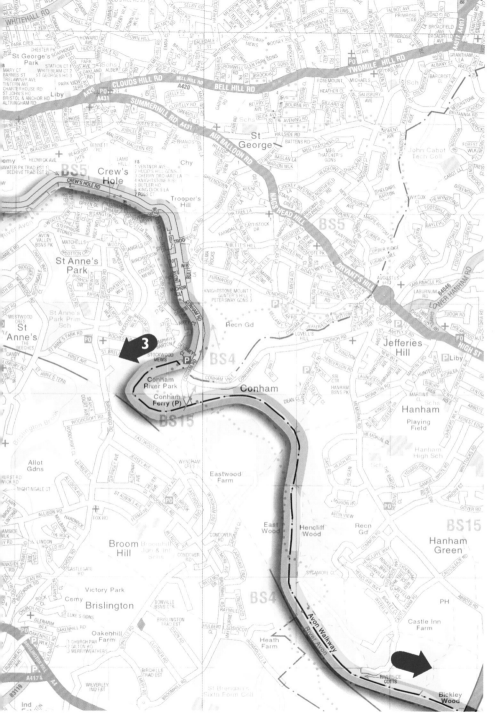

Leave the tarmac at Conham River Park, and follow the riverside bridleway for 4km to Hanham Lock

4 Leave the riverside path, left, up the steep lane (Ferry Road). At the T-junction at the end, go right (Court Farm Road). Continue (climbing) for 1.5km, and turn right on the main A431 Bath Road.

Drop down and head up past Willsbridge Mill to the roundabout, and go left (Bath Road) signed for the Railway Path. After 400m, reach Bitton station (the railway path crosses the road on the bridge above).

5 Join the Bristol & Bath Railway Path (NCN4) going left, north (past the station alongside the station car park).

Continue for 12km, following signs to Bristol (several junctions, for features see full railway path Route 3), all the way to the end of the path, where you approach the city centre.

Stay with the cycle route on the road, following signs: St Philip's Street/Midland Road/Horton Street. Follow the route across the dramatic contemporary pedestrian bridge at Temple Quay – please walk and give way to pedestrians on this popular crossing.

Continue left through the modern square, towards Temple Meads station buildings. There, go on foot into the train shed. The footway exit lies 100m right down the shed.

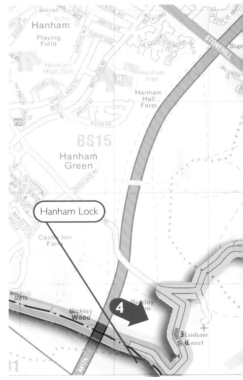

38

Bristol and Bath Railway Path

Bitton Station

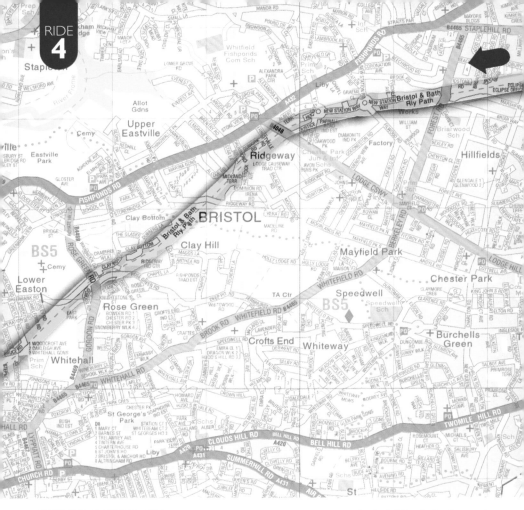

Right: Leave the river, past two pubs, at Hanham Lock. Left: The riverside bridleway is very scenic — but does flood after exceptional rainfall.

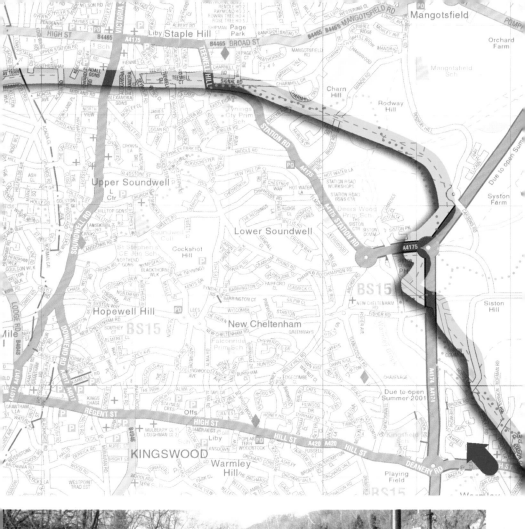

Bristol North: Fishponds to Iron Acton

An intriguing circuit of cycle paths and lanes that leaves the suburbs for the country, from Fishponds to rural Iron Acton, and returns via the University of the West of England and Frenchay Common.

This escape route north from the city to the countryside has pretty touches and an exploratory feel. The circuit connects northeast Bristol suburbs with the country pubs of Iron Acton, much of it on cycle routing, much of that car-free. From Fishponds (although you can start anywhere) the first 5km follows the Bristol & Bath Railway Path and branch-line out to Shortwood. We then follow the Avon Cycleway on lanes through Frampton Cotterell for 6km out to rural Iron Acton.

Turning back south, after 4km more Avon Cycleway, pass close to Parkway station then, on cycle paths beside the university to

RIDE INFORMATION

Distance	30km (19 miles)
Car-free	8km (5 miles) (26%)
Grade	Easy-moderate, it is quite long and fiddly in places, with rises

Suitability for children and occasional riders?
In part yes. Good sections include the Bristol & Bath Railway Path and continuation out to Shortwood, while the paths around the University of the West of England (UWE) are clear. But the full distance is too much, and there are a small number of stretches with traffic and hills.

Start/finish and parking
Start anywhere en route. We choose the Bristol & Bath Railway Path at Fishponds (adjoining the Safeway car park/Hockey Road off Fishponds Road)

Literature
The Bristol & Bath Railway Path leaflet (Bristol City Council tel: 0117 903 6827); Sustrans map/*Route NCN4* (tel: 0117 929 0888); *Avon Cycleway* leaflet (137km circular road ride around Bristol & Bath, free, Bristol City Council tel: 0117 903 6842); *Cycling to Work in North Bristol* (free, Bristol City Council tel: 0117 903 6842 and South Gloucestershire Council tel: 01454 863748)

Refreshments
The Bridge pub in Shortwood; the Rose & Crown (traditional, real ale) and the White Hart (aka the Hungry Horse, family pub with outside tables) in Iron Acton

What to see
Interesting buildings include Acton Court north of Acton, but this is not open to the public

Above: Leave the city behind on the lanes to Iron Acton. Below: Iron Acton village green – start of the return leg.

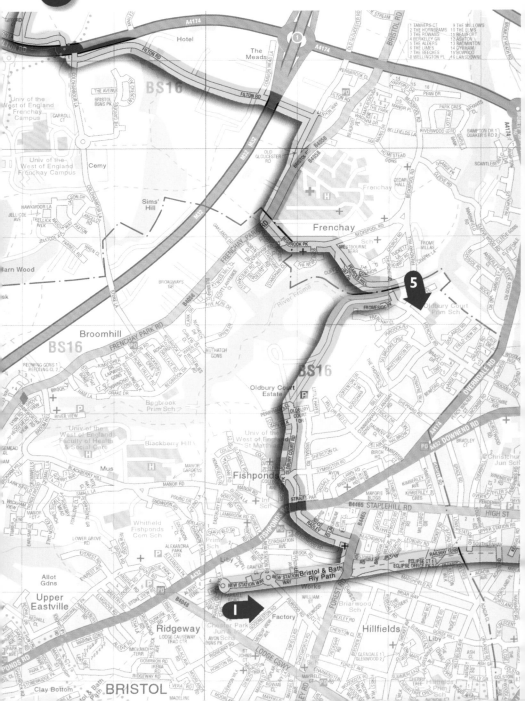

RIDE
5

Frenchay. Continue past attractive Frenchay Common, drop steeply to the river Frome, and ride through Oldbury Court Estate.

The most pleasant sections are the Railway Path, the lane to Iron Acton, Frenchay and Oldbury Court. While you are kept away from the traffic most the of the time, the B4059 at the north end turnaround point between Iron Acton and Earthcott Green carries occasional fast traffic and lorries, but is quieter at weekends.

❶ *Join the Bristol & Bath Railway Path (NCN4) beside the Safeway car park at Hockeys Lane, off Fishponds Road. Head eastward (left from the car park, uphill) for 3km (including Staple Hill Tunnel) to the junction at* old Mangotsfield station. Fork left signed Avon Cycleway North to Frampton Cotterell (NCN4 to Bath goes right) and continue along the old railway line for 800m.

Continue beside the A4174 Avon Ring Road for 1km (after 400m the Bridge Inn lies over the roadbridge cycleway) as far as the roundabout.

Proceed beneath the subway and on the far side go left rising (Avon Cycleway North, Frampton Cotterell) and at the top continue on the straight-ahead railway path to Frampton Cotterell. (On the left, continuing beside the ring road, is an alternative route that rejoins at Henfield.)

Continue for 1km on the tarmac path to the end where the tarmac runs down right beside the bridge embankment to the lane (the railway line path continues unsurfaced).

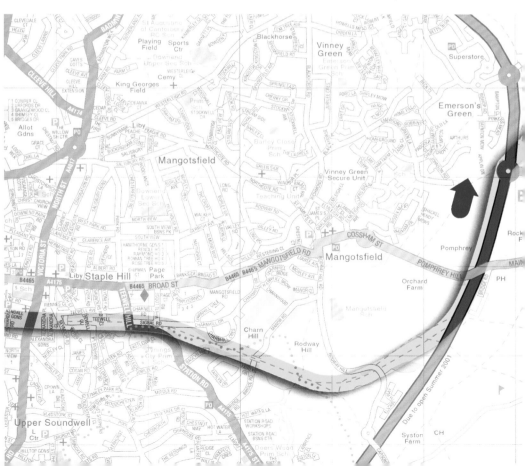

2 We now follow the Avon Cycleway as far as Iron Acton. Go left beneath the railway bridge (signed for Coalpit Heath) and continue on this lane for 800m. Ride straight over the crossroads, and continue as far as the T-junction in Coalpit Heath. Turn right (signed for Yate), ride up Roundways and then go left into South View Rise, and right very soon into South View Crescent. At the end, cross straight over the main road carefully (pedestrian lights) and continue into Woodend Road. Bear right at the end, staying in Woodend Road/Lower Stone Close.

At the end, dogleg left/right (Church Road/Frampton End Road) to ride in the same direction on the little lane. After 1.5km join the bigger road to bear right into Iron Acton. (In the village the Hungry Horse pub is on your left, the Rose & Crown along the High Street going off right.)

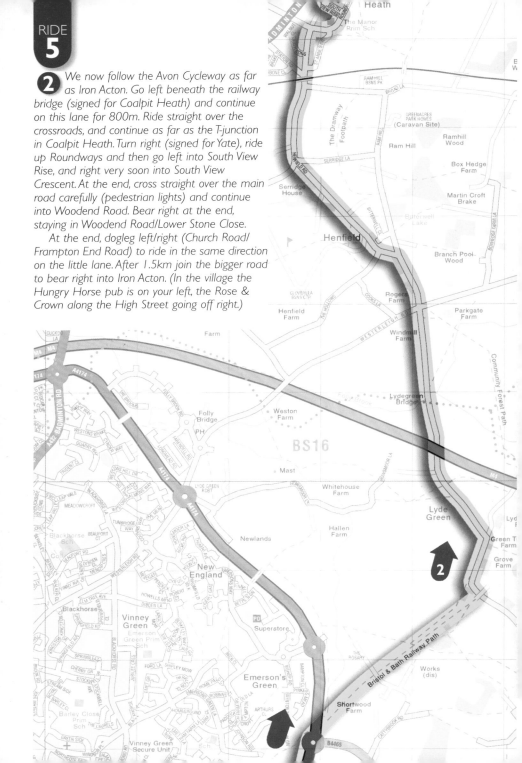

3 Continue to the traffic lights, and go straight over (to Latteridge) and continue on this road (B4059) for 3km through Latteridge to Earthcott Green. Watch for the occasional fast car and lorry. At Earthcott, go left (to Hambrook) on the B4427, the Old Gloucester Road, and continue for 4.5km, passing at the end over the M5 to the T-junction with the dual-carriageway B4057.

In Bristol, the countryside is never far away.

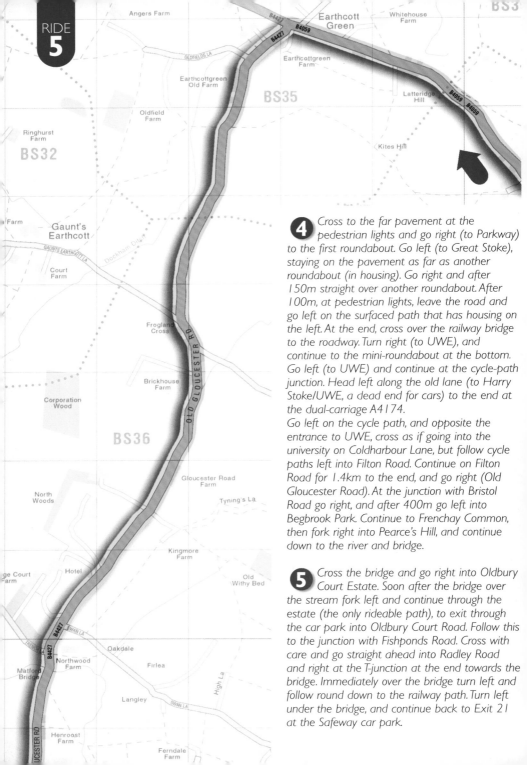

RIDE

5

4 Cross to the far pavement at the pedestrian lights and go right (to Parkway) to the first roundabout. Go left (to Great Stoke), staying on the pavement as far as another roundabout (in housing). Go right and after 150m straight over another roundabout. After 100m, at pedestrian lights, leave the road and go left on the surfaced path that has housing on the left. At the end, cross over the railway bridge to the roadway. Turn right (to UWE), and continue to the mini-roundabout at the bottom. Go left (to UWE) and continue at the cycle-path junction. Head left along the old lane (to Harry Stoke/UWE, a dead end for cars) to the end at the dual-carriage A4174.
Go left on the cycle path, and opposite the entrance to UWE, cross as if going into the university on Coldharbour Lane, but follow cycle paths left into Filton Road. Continue on Filton Road for 1.4km to the end, and go right (Old Gloucester Road). At the junction with Bristol Road go right, and after 400m go left into Begbrook Park. Continue to Frenchay Common, then fork right into Pearce's Hill, and continue down to the river and bridge.

5 Cross the bridge and go right into Oldbury Court Estate. Soon after the bridge over the stream fork left and continue through the estate (the only rideable path), to exit through the car park into Oldbury Court Road. Follow this to the junction with Fishponds Road. Cross with care and go straight ahead into Radley Road and right at the T-junction at the end towards the bridge. Immediately over the bridge turn left and follow round down to the railway path. Turn left under the bridge, and continue back to Exit 21 at the Safeway car park.

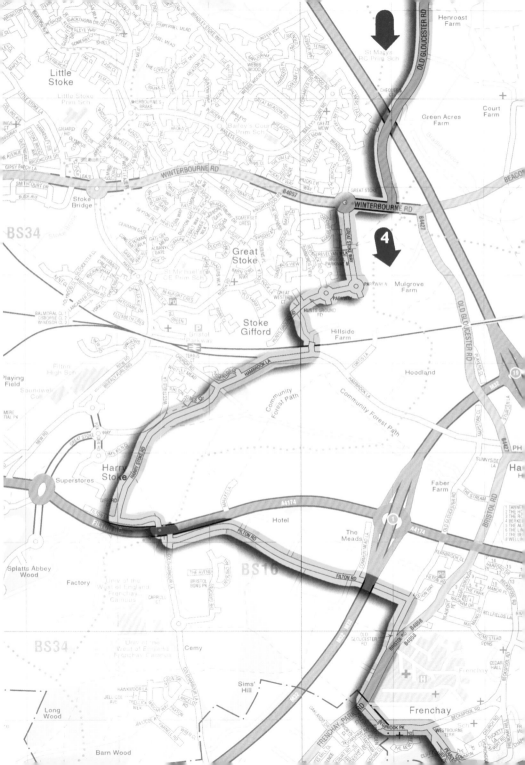

Severn Bridges tour on lanes

A short way north of Bristol, the low-lying landscape beside the two Severn bridgeheads is rural and pretty in summer. The seafront at Severn Beach and Old Passage offer spectacular views. Trains to the two stations en route are scarce, so plan your transport carefully.

Ride on a clement Saturday and the gentle landscape and expansive views of the Severn estuary and bridges make this a memorable trip out from Bristol by train (see Stations, and ring Wessex Trains for details).

From the flat banks, the two bridges, the original, northerly 1960s suspension bridge and the southerly 1990s French-designed M4 crossing are lofty giants visible for miles. The older bridge bears a segregated cycle route which you can take for mid-channel views or even follow (continuing on a Sustrans-signed cycle route) to the attractive castle town of Chepstow on the banks of the River Wye (12km return from English start of bridge).

RIDE INFORMATION

Distance 25km (16 miles)
Car-free 1.5km (1 mile) (6%)
Grade Easy (flat, but you need good weather)

Suitability for children and occasional riders
Good for older children and casual cyclists, as the traffic is light and the terrain flat, but make sure the day is calm – you don't want a headwind heading southwest

Traffic
Lightly trafficked lanes or segregated cycle paths throughout (right-hand town turns in Olveston and Easter Compton)

Start/finish
Severn Beach station

Stations
Severn Beach (reserve 24 hours ahead to 'guarantee' a bike space; weekdays four direct early morning/evening trains from Bristol Temple Meads. (There is a bus service from Avonmouth to Severn Beach throughout the rest of the day but it doesn't carry bikes.) Saturdays, approximately hourly direct service; no Sunday service (Wessex Trains tel: 08456 000880); (Pilning has an awkward, single daily service)

Literature
The route map and details of NCN4 (from Sustrans), and the Avon Cycleway map

Refreshments
The White Horse near Pilning; Severn View Services (old Severn Bridge Aust Services); the Plough Inn near Pilning station; pubs in Olveston and Easter Compton

What to see
The original and later road bridges crossing the broad River Severn estuary over to Wales (but ignore signs for a visitor centre – it's closed)

This route offers fine views of the two great estuary crossings: here the M4 bridge.

Much of the riding is on country lanes, the nicest stretch being between Olveston and Marsh Common, where reeds grow in the fenland ditches. There is a short section of road with more traffic coming into Easter Compton.

One section, Dyer's Common, between the M49 motorway and the industrial estate on the outskirts of Severn Beach, may be diverted in the future due to problems with tipping.

Much of the route uses parts of the Avon Cycleway and NCN4 (Bristol to Gloucester). You could follow the latter out via the Avon Gorge, by-passing Avonmouth and following roads to Severn Beach, make the ride and return by train, but check the train times carefully. The route is also within easy reach of the northern suburbs of Patchway, Filton, Henbury and Lawrence Weston.

Despite its striking seafront, Severn Beach is very quiet, so don't leave yourself time to kill here unless the weather is good. A nice pub nearby is the White Horse 2km along the route, which could be another start/finish point if you are driving there.

RIDE
6

The newer M4 bridge

White Horse pub

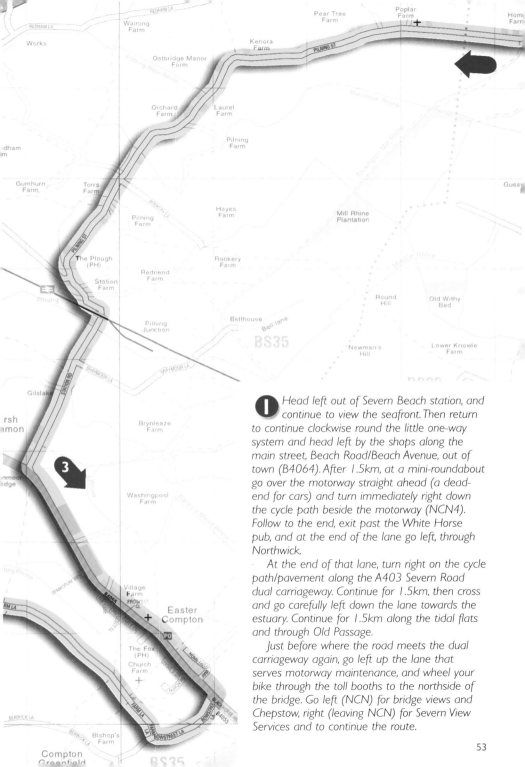

1 Head left out of Severn Beach station, and continue to view the seafront. Then return to continue clockwise round the little one-way system and head left by the shops along the main street, Beach Road/Beach Avenue, out of town (B4064). After 1.5km, at a mini-roundabout go over the motorway straight ahead (a dead-end for cars) and turn immediately right down the cycle path beside the motorway (NCN4). Follow to the end, exit past the White Horse pub, and at the end of the lane go left, through Northwick.

At the end of that lane, turn right on the cycle path/pavement along the A403 Severn Road dual carriageway. Continue for 1.5km, then cross and go carefully left down the lane towards the estuary. Continue for 1.5km along the tidal flats and through Old Passage.

Just before where the road meets the dual carriageway again, go left up the lane that serves motorway maintenance, and wheel your bike through the toll booths to the northside of the bridge. Go left (NCN) for bridge views and Chepstow, right (leaving NCN) for Severn View Services and to continue the route.

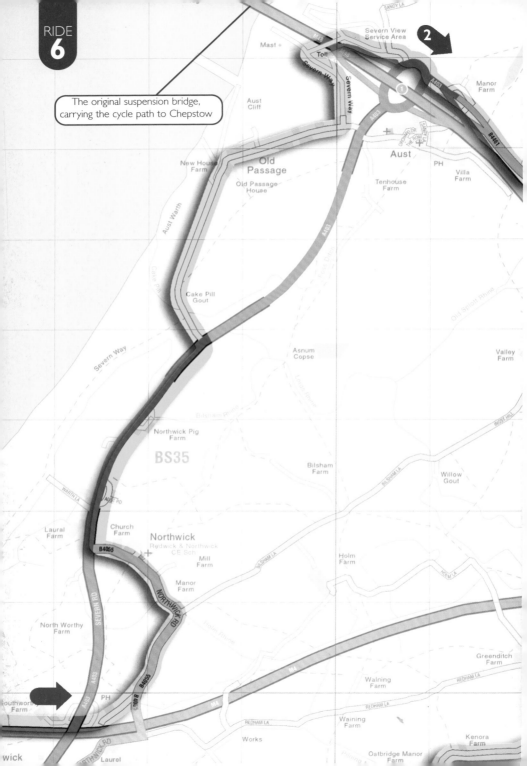

RIDE
6

The original suspension bridge,
carrying the cycle path to Chepstow

2

SANDY LA

Severn View
Service Area

A48

Toll

Severn Way

Severn Way

Mast

①

A403

Manor
Farm

Aust
Cliff

A403

B4461

SANDY LA

ORCHARD DR

Aust

PH

Villa
Farm

New House
Farm

**Old
Passage**

Old Passage
House

A403

Tenhouse
Farm

Villa
Farm

Aust Warth

Cross Drain

Valley
Farm

Cake Pill

Cake Pill
Gout

Asnum
Copse

Old Splott Rhine

Severn Way

Cross Rhine

Bilsham Rhine

AUST HILL

Northwick Pig
Farm

BS35

Bilsham
Farm

BILSHAM LA

Willow
Gout

WARTH RD

AUST RD

Laural
Farm

Church
Farm

Northwick

Redwick & Northwick
CE Sch

B4055

Mill
Farm

BILSHAM LA

Holm
Farm

HOLM LA

SEVERN RD

NORTHWICK RD

Manor
Farm

Holm Rhine

North Worthy
Farm

A403

B4055

M4

Greenditch
Farm

PH

Walning
Farm

REDHAM LA

wick

NORTHWICK RD

Laurel

REDHAM LA

Works

Waining
Farm

Ostbridge Manor
Farm

Kenora
Farm

2 Exit the services carefully and at the roundabout take the first sliproad (for London and M42). Stay left and at the top take the Thornbury road, B4461. Continue 1.3km, then turn off (straight ahead where the road bends left) to Olveston. Continue 2km, then in Olveston, where we pick up the Avon Cycleway, go right by the Post Office. Continue through the village (signed Awkley and Pilning) and out over two motorway bridges. Turn left into Awkley Lane and continue for 600m to crossroads. Go right, westward, and continue for 4km, past Pilning station, to the end of the road.

Right and below: The newer southern crossing, and the expansive seafront and promenade at Severn Beach.

The original Severn Bridge to the north. A
segregated cycle path continues across to Chepstow.

3 Turn left on the B4055 (the busiest road of the route) 1.6km to Easter Compton. Through the village go right down Bowstreet Lane, and after 300m go right into Farm Lane, turning northwest back towards the estuary.

This lane continues over the M49 motorway, then deteriorates to nothing. Continue down the lane, picking up the NCN cycle path and proceed through the new industrial estate. Stay in the same direction with NCN, crossing the A403, following a simple pathway and emerging on a residential road. Go left at the end signed to Severn Beach. At the end, dogleg left/right into Station Road back to the station.

RIDE
7

Yate to the
Cotswold fringe on lanes

Reach the lovely villages of Horton and Hawkesbury in the Cotswold foothills on this easy ride through mellow countryside around Yate.

Yate, lying to the north of Bristol and Bath, is within easy bike-striking distance of the Cotswold foothills just 8km away. This ride is accessible for Bristolians, who can travel by train directly to the town from both Temple Meads and Parkway. Bath residents must cycle out or drive. Most of the route follows the Avon Cycleway, with the advantage of signposting and the best of the lanes (see Literature).

This is a peaceful route over the agricultural plain to the Cotswold escarpment at Horton. Here, halfway up the rise, is the stately Horton Court, a National Trust

RIDE INFORMATION

Distance	30km (19 miles)
Grade	Easy (with two sub-1km climbs)

Suitability for children and occasional riders?
Yes, the distance, traffic level and two paced hills make this good for older children and occasional cyclists who still ride every so often

Start/finish
Yate station

Traffic
Once you have left Yate, traffic is light on the lanes. On the return, there is 4km on the B4058 much of which is pavement cycle path, avoiding the infrequent fast traffic and lorries

Stations
Yate (from Bristol Temple Meads, 25 minute journey time, seven trains Saturday, no Sunday service; trains runs via Bristol Parkway; no direct service from Bath Spa). Bikes on trains (Wessex Trains customer

service tel: 0845 600 0880); bikes are carried offpeak free on a first-come-first-served basis (maximum two bikes) at the conductor's discretion

Literature
Ordnance Survey *Landranger map 31*; map of the *Avon Cycleway* (137km circular road ride around Bristol & Bath) free from Bristol City Council tel: 0117 903 6842

Refreshments
Pubs and stores in Yate and Wickwar; Wickwar Tearooms; but nothing particularly stands out en route

Bike shops
Yate – Terry's Cycles, Station Road (close to station, tel: 01454 318938), Halfords in town shopping centre (tel: 01454 318671)

Things to see
Horton Court (tel: 01249 730141, open April-October, National Trust) lies 9km from the start (beautifully sited, but the hall is in ruins; the house is closed to the public); villages of Horton and Hawkesbury

property, which features the remains of a Norman hall and fine detached ambulatory (cloister) – but no tearoom unluckily for us! (The house is closed to the public.)

The halfway-up lane from here along the escarpment to Hawkesbury is one of the nicest. Thereafter we climb a combe to the top, to the ancient drovers pool at the Hawkesbury Upton road. On past the memorial, back down on the plain we cross atmospheric Inglestone Common, complete with cattle grids and timeless looks.

Beyond Wickwar, which has a typical semi-handsome high street and shops, we meet the B4058 but are saved from the full jolt back into the 21st century by a pavement cyclepath much of the way. Continue to the point where we left Yate, for the return to the station.

The two hills are both tolerable by occasional riders; a 50m rise in 500m in Horton and a 70m rise in 1km at Hawkesbury to the pool (soon followed by a nice descent).

Above: Leave Yate behind on pretty lanes. Right: The prettiness of the Cotswolds shows through on the lane to Horton Court.

1 From Yate station, go right on the main road over the railway bridge, and take the first right, North Road. Continue more or less in this direction for 2.5km, over a crossroads (signed dead-end for cars), through cycle bollards across the ring road (signed for Council Offices, North Road), out of town, to a lane junction where this road bends left and a minor lane goes off perpendicular, right.

2 Go right here on Tan House Lane (signed for Yate Rocks). Continue 2.5km to the crossroads with the B4060, and go straight over, Mapleridge Lane. Continue 2.5km to the T-junction, and turn left down to Horton. Continue through the village, and take the second left up the hill signed for Horton Court and Hawkesbury (not first left, King Lane; the cycleway signpost seems to be wrong).

3 After Horton, continue (now travelling north) for 2.5km, and go right at the lane T-junction into Hawkesbury. Carry on up the combe, to the drovers pool at the top beside the major road. Go left on the major road (signed for Wickwar). At the monument after 350m, turn left (signed for Wickwar) and descend steeply back to the plain.

At Inglestone Common continue (signed to Wickwar). Continue for 4.5km, across the common, to the T-junction in Wickwar.

4 Here in Wickwar, go left, and just before the traffic lights, head right on the B4509 (signed to Charfield). After 300m turn left on a minor lane (signed to West End and Cromhall).

At West End, continue to Cromhall. At the T-junction with the B4058, go left (signed to Rangeworthy). Continue for 4km, much of it pavement cycle path, to the left turn on to minor Manor Road (not the one to Wickwar, or the dead-end Patch Lane).

Continue on Manor Road back to our outward point, and retrace your steps back to Yate station.

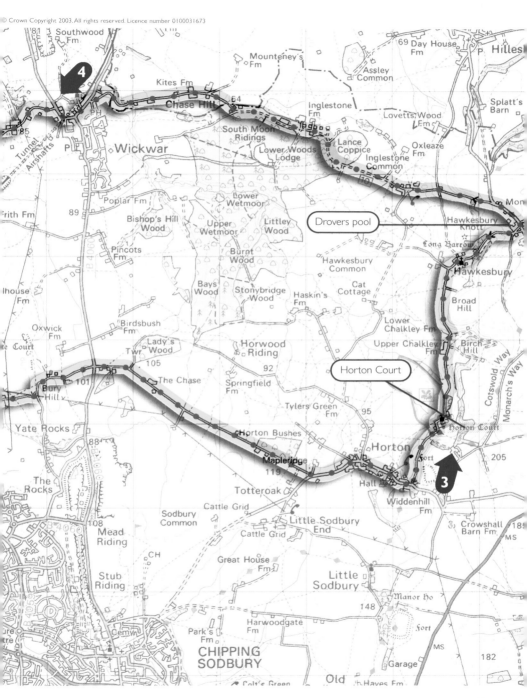

© Crown Copyright 2003. All rights reserved. Licence number 0100031673

Drovers pool

Horton Court

61

Bristol Ashton Court

to Clevedon Seafront on rural lanes

Fine country lanes lead from Bristol through the tranquil Gordano Valley to Clevedon and back via levels to Brockley Combe and Long Ashton.

This scenic circuit from Bristol to the sea follows fine lanes, has good views and hits a seaside resort for lunch. It's full of short hills, and you will feel it in your legs at the end of the day – excellent for gently pushing your fitness!

RIDE INFORMATION

Distance	46km (29 miles)
Car-free	1km (2/3 mile) in Ashton Court
Grade	Moderate-difficult (it is lengthy, with dozens of rises)

Suitability for children and occasional riders?
Not really, because of the length and rises

Traffic
The opening 2km on the A369 carries fast traffic and narrows down through Abbots Leigh; also 2km on the busy A38 between Bristol airport and Barrow Gurney (return leg)

Start/finish
Clifton Suspension Bridge or Ashton Court Leigh Woods entrance (parking)

Stations
Yatton (4km southeast of Clevedon); Nailsea (both to Bristol Temple Meads)

Refreshments
Cafe at Ashton Court; village pubs on the way – the Priory in Portbury; the Black Horse in Clapton in Gordano; Moon & Sixpence on Clevedon seafront; the Blue Flame Inn at West End (near Nailsea)

Literature
This partly follows the Avon Cycleway (137km circular road ride around Bristol and Bath, free from Bristol City Council tel: 0117 903 6842)

Bike shops
Bristol – see Route 1; Clevedon – Bike King, 19 Old Street (tel: 01275 873551), Bike Style, Tweed Road (tel: 01275 335822).

Nailsea – Nailsea Cycles, 6 Clevedon Walk (tel: 01275 858000) and 132 High Street (tel: 01275 855800)

What to see
Clevedon pier, promenade and sea bathing pool; Clevedon Court (outstanding 14th century manor house, National Trust, open Apr-Nov); toads migrating over Clevedon Lane at night

Clevedon makes a good turnaround point, with its beach and cafes.

In season toads migrate across Clevedon Lane to breed in the rhynes (ditches) of the Gordano Valley.

Within five minutes of setting off from Ashton Court, you are in hilly lanes as far as Portbury. This is the pick-up point for the sweet little road – Clevedon Lane – that contours along the rural Gordano Valley virtually to Clevedon. Most people view the valley at high speed from the M5, but spinning easily along on the bike you get the essential impression of gentle slopes, settlements and farmland.

Genteel Clevedon has a bandstand, pier and promenade, seafront cafes and benches overlooking the wide Severn estuary – a pleasant place to soak up the sun awhile. You could also break for a visit to Clevedon Court on the outskirts, a renowned National Trust property (entry fee, no cafe).

Head back across the levels around Nailsea and up the wooded mini-gorge of Brockley Combe – a comfortably steady climb. Emerge near the control tower and terminal at Bristol airport, and then go heads-down on a short but noisy stretch on the A38 for 2km. At the end of elongated Long Ashton, you will find yourself opposite the lower entrance of Ashton Court.

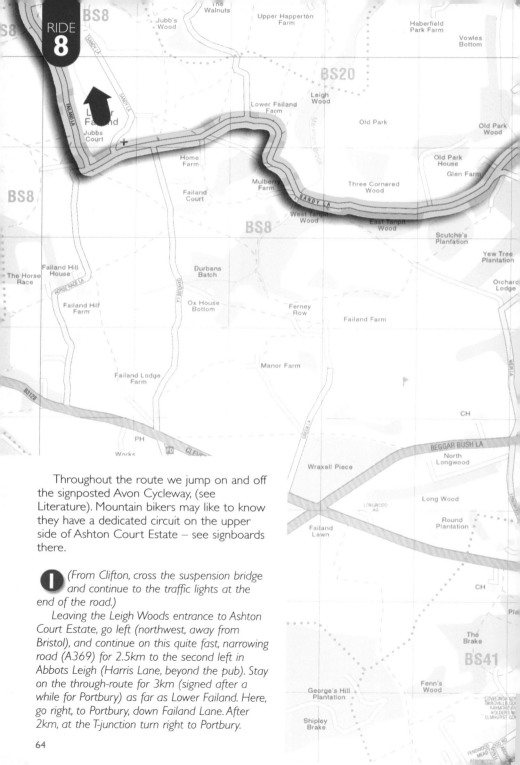

Throughout the route we jump on and off the signposted Avon Cycleway, (see Literature). Mountain bikers may like to know they have a dedicated circuit on the upper side of Ashton Court Estate – see signboards there.

1 *(From Clifton, cross the suspension bridge and continue to the traffic lights at the end of the road.)*

Leaving the Leigh Woods entrance to Ashton Court Estate, go left (northwest, away from Bristol), and continue on this quite fast, narrowing road (A369) for 2.5km to the second left in Abbots Leigh (Harris Lane, beyond the pub). Stay on the through-route for 3km (signed after a while for Portbury) as far as Lower Failand. Here, go right, to Portbury, down Failand Lane. After 2km, at the T-junction turn right to Portbury.

2 In Portbury, go left at the T-junction, and then straight on (to Clapton, Avon Cycleway) where the road bends right. Continue under the motorway bridge (not left before, to Nailsea), into the Gordano Valley, and at the T-junction go right, down Naish Hill, into Clapton in Gordano. Here, turn left into Clevedon Lane, signed for Clapton Wick and Clevedon, and continue for 6km (to the outskirts of Clevedon).

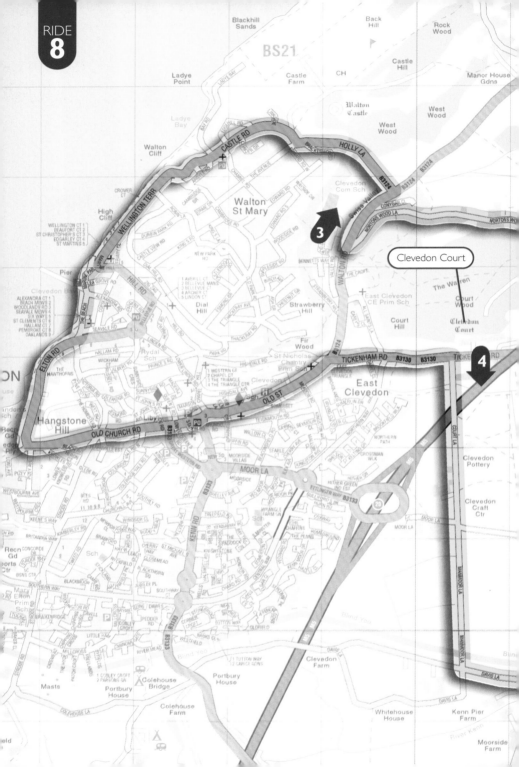

BS21

Clevedon Court

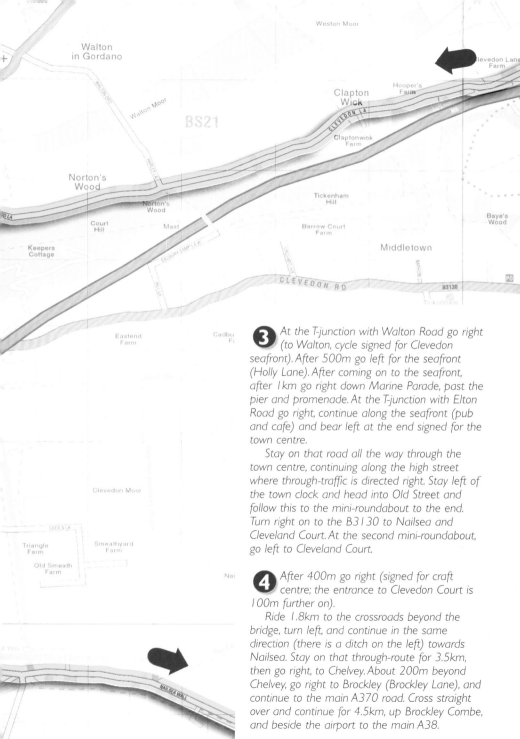

3 At the T-junction with Walton Road go right (to Walton, cycle signed for Clevedon seafront). After 500m go left for the seafront (Holly Lane). After coming on to the seafront, after 1km go right down Marine Parade, past the pier and promenade. At the T-junction with Elton Road go right, continue along the seafront (pub and cafe) and bear left at the end signed for the town centre.

Stay on that road all the way through the town centre, continuing along the high street where through-traffic is directed right. Stay left of the town clock and head into Old Street and follow this to the mini-roundabout to the end. Turn right on to the B3130 to Nailsea and Cleveland Court. At the second mini-roundabout, go left to Cleveland Court.

4 After 400m go right (signed for craft centre; the entrance to Clevedon Court is 100m further on).

Ride 1.8km to the crossroads beyond the bridge, turn left, and continue in the same direction (there is a ditch on the left) towards Nailsea. Stay on that through-route for 3.5km, then go right, to Chelvey. About 200m beyond Chelvey, go right to Brockley (Brockley Lane), and continue to the main A370 road. Cross straight over and continue for 4.5km, up Brockley Combe, and beside the airport to the main A38.

NAILSEA

Backwell

Backwell
Common

Backwell

West
Town

5 Go left on the A38 (to Bristol), and ride mindful of heavy traffic for 2km, where, going downhill (150m beyond the Fox & Goose pub on the right), you turn left, up little Hobbs Lane (Avon Cycleway, barriered to cars). At Barrow Gurney at the bottom, cross carefully straight over, and up the steep, rough (thankfully short) track opposite. Go straight ahead on the joining lane at the top, and continue to the T-junction in Long Ashton. Head right along Weston Road, through Long Ashton and at the end, the junction with the B3128, go straight ahead into Ashton Court Estate. Continue on and up the track, bearing left near the house itself (where there's a cafe), and right, back round to the

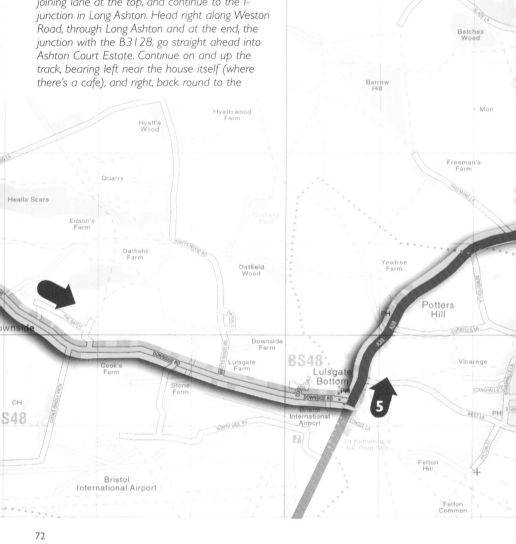

The Fillies

Ridings Wood

Barrow

Crossgrove Wood

WILD COUNTRY LA

Barrow Mill

Barrow Wood

The Wild Country

BS48

School Farm

BS48

BARROW ST

SCHOOL LA

Church Wood

Barrow Big Wood

Monarch's Way

Dead Hill Wood

Barrow Gurney

PO

MAIN ST

Steps Farm

MAIN LA

Water Works

BS130

A38 A38

Barrow Common

Greenditch Farm

Stevens' Farm

Hill Farm

Stevens' Wood

BS130

KINGS LA

Dial Farm

SHAM LA

PH

Glenville House Farm

BRIDGWATER RD

BARROW LA

Castle Farm

Hartcliff Rocks

ROCKS LA

BS40

ELWELL LA

ELWELL LA

BS40

Felton

BURRELLS LA

HELTON LA

FROG LA

STANSHALLS DR

New Farm

Upper Town

PO

ORCHARD DR

Hanging Grove Farm

Grove Farm

B3130

BARROW LA

DUNDRY LA

Monarch's Way

Long Cross

VEE LA

LONG CROSS

BINEGAR LA

KINGSTON LA

FELTON LA

KINGSTON MEAD

BARROW LA

BROOK LA

Hayes Cottage

Oldhill Farm

Winford CE Prim Sch

HIGH ST

Winford

CHURCH RD

CHURCH RISE

PO

CHAPEL

B3130

Kentshre

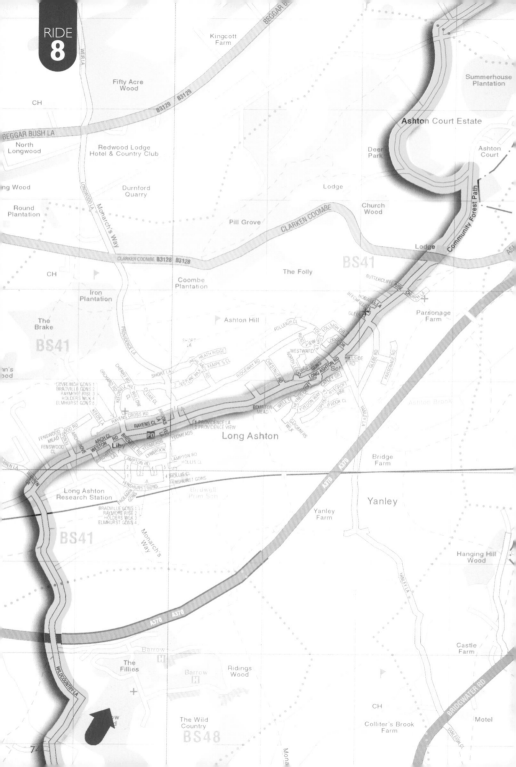

Views of seafront Victoriana at Clevedon.

Bristol Southwest MTB: Ashton Court to Dundry

A handsome, hilly mountain bike ride that borders the city and peaks with the best views of Bristol. Travel on the Ashton Court MTB route via idyllic Bourton Combe to hilltop Dundry, and return on the urban Malago Greenway.

This route may not appear to offer much, but it contains a meritable amount of climbing on rough tracks and is worthy of the Bristol off-road fraternity, yet you are never more than 5km west of the city limits.

From Ashton Court you ascend in waves accompanied by longer and longer views all the way up to the Dundry summit. You need

RIDE INFORMATION

Distance 24km (15 miles)
Car-free 15km (9 miles) (60%)

Grade
Difficult mountain bike route to suit regular riders (it may look short, but there are plenty of rough uphill tracks, slower in wet conditions)

Suitability for children and occasional riders?
Nope

Traffic
Road crossings and short sections on road with fast traffic; the B3128 (bordering Ashton Court); a narrow 1km on the A370 to Flax Bourton; a staggered crossing of the A38 towards Dundry; and watch out crossing on a blind corner on the B3130 closer to Dundry, the Malago Greenway has road links

Start/finish
Start at Clifton Lodge upper entrance of

Ashton Court Estate (off A369 – opposite Bridge Road to Clifton Suspension Bridge); finish in Windmill Hill at a cycle route junction that leads either to the centre or Totterdown

Stations
Bristol Temple Meads; Bedminster

Refreshments
The cafe at Ashton Court; the Jubilee Inn in Flax Bourton; the Dundry Inn and the Carpenters Inn in Dundry

Bike shops
Central Bristol: Dave Bater Cycles at the bottom of Park Street (tel: 0117 929 7368); Mud Dock Cycleworks (tel: 0117 929 2151) near the Arnolfini

What to see
Ashton Court visitor centre (a little below the route start, tel: 0117 963 9174)

to be fit to enjoy it, and after wet weather the going gets hard in a couple of places. A challenge is to ride all the way without a dab. Please shut all gates in this working farmland, and carry a puncture kit against the brambles and hawthorns.

We start by doing half of the rather good Ashton Court MTB circuit (which is worth completing another day, especially as the house has a cafe for post-ride repast), then head out to Failand on the road, for a cute downhill bridleway to an unexpected waterside beauty spot – where after rain Eeyore would be in heaven. On the far side of Flax Bourton, there's a choice of three fine bridleways up Bourton Combe, a steep wooded dell. We take the eastside track, which has the gentlest gradient, a good surface and the least sunny aspect. The other two are

steeper, but all emerge at the same spot. When the route was ridden we had to walk the rutted RUPP (road used a a public path) on Barrow Hill, which filled the bike with mud immediately. Hopefully in dry weather, you will pass without noticing.

The biggest climb and technical challenge is the last stony zig-zag bridleway climb of 90m to Dundry (233m). The village overlooks most of Bristol, and its ornate church tower is a landmark visible for miles around.

We drop down through the suburbs partly on the Malago Greenway, a stout, council attempt to upgrade an urban green corridor. The signing and paths are of good standard but the environment is blighted in places (see Route 6 for more). We quit at Windmill Hill, where the route is signed to both the city centre and Totterdown; over to you.

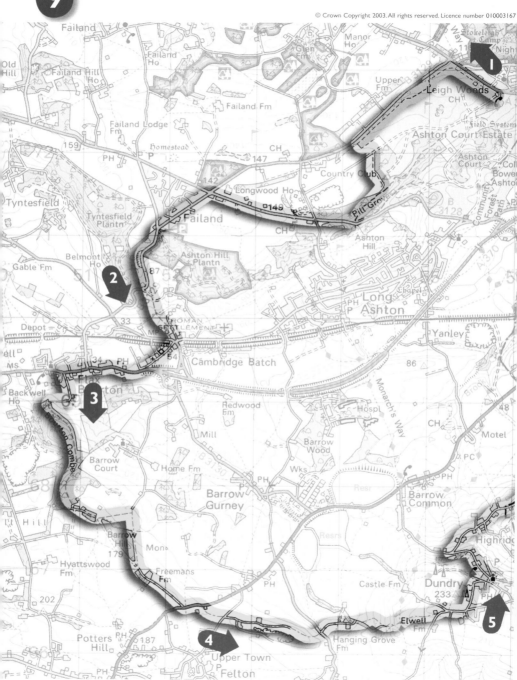

© Crown Copyright 2003. All rights reserved. Licence number 010003167

1 From Clifton Lodge, the upper entrance of Ashton Court Estate (near the suspension bridge), follow the dirt MTB course uphill (northwest), immediately right if you come through the lodge. Follow the clear wooded singletrack for 2km around the wall, and left across open fields to a gravel track. Cross, run beside the wire fence, and go right after 150m at the gravel bridleway (marked with white posts).

At the track T-junction at the bottom, go right on the bridleway. Turn right at the first fork, and left at the second (bridleway). There is a sharp left-hand corner at the bottom of that track beside the road, exit the estate here, through the gap in the stone wall. Head right, uphill on the road (B3128). Continue for 1.9km to Failand, go left (for Weston) on the B3129 and continue for 1.8km, descending. At the start of a right-hand curve, look for the bridleway set back from the road (there is no path from the road; if you miss it, continue to the lane on the left where the roads straightens out, and pick up the bridleway a little lower down).

2 Follow the bridleway down the field to exit at the gravel track, and opposite, take the double-track through the gate in the same direction. At the bottom (a beauty spot, which may be wet, but is lovely in summer), cross the stream and make your way up the bridleway on the far side. This becomes a lane (go right) that finishes at the double mini-roundabouts.

Take the minor road at 2 o'clock off the right-hand mini-roundabout, to the Magistrates Court. After 300m, fork left towards the main road (A370). Go carefully right on the road towards Flax Bourton (narrows) and continue for 1km.

3 After 1km, go left up a lane, Bourton Combe, and right at the top (bridleway). Soon, at the bridleway junction, turn 90 degrees up left (for other bridleways you can also either continue or go right off the route after 150m – all emerge at the same point). At the top, pass the farmstead and head through the metal gate on to the lane. Continue to the common, and go left (bridleway) and soon, beside two metal gates, right on a RUPP (two sides of a triangle)

(Barrow Hill). At the crosstracks at the trees, continue straight ahead for 600m (bad after rain). Pass through the metal gate at the end, head to the top left of the field, and exit on a lane that finishes at the busy A38.

4 Go left with care and after 400m, cross the road carefully, to find a RUPP through the Bridle Cottage B&B. Continue on this track to lanes, and go straight ahead on the quarry road, and down to meet the B3130. Cross carefully straight over on this blind corner. Continue to the end of the surfacing and up the rough climbing RUPP (accompanied by the waters of Elwell spring).

Stay straight ahead at the top across fields to the lane, and continue on that in the same direction. After 400m turn left, signed for Dundry.

The Ashton Court MTB course starts with flowing, twisting singletrack.

© Crown Copyright 2003. All rights reserved. Licence number 0100031673

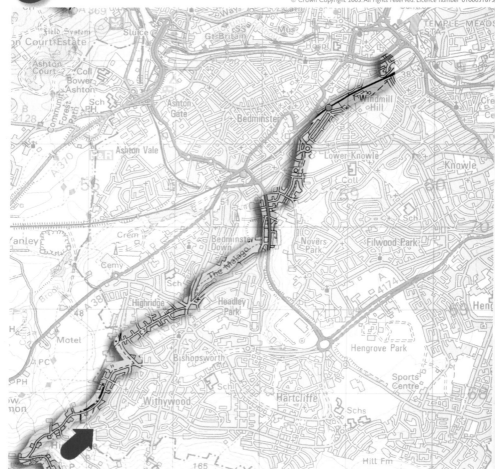

5 Past Dundry Down, in the village, go left in front of the church, and left again (Dundry Lane) downhill. After 600m, turn right, signed for Bishopsworth, down Highridge Road. Continue for 2km to Highridge Common. Go left at the end of the common into Highridge Green (two sides of the common). On the right-hand bend towards the end of the grass, go right down Sandburrows Road (signed for the schools). Continue to the end, Bishopsworth Road (signed for Malago Greenway) and dogleg left/right into St Peter's Rise. Immediately, pick up the riverside Malago Greenway path on the left (a stream is on your right). The Greenway is now signed into the centre.

After 1km, emerge on the main A4174 Hartcliffe Way. Go left (the opposite pavement is a shared cycle path) and after 300m, cross at the cycle lights, follow that side of the road, and soon go right into Hastings Road, then right into Parson Street and pick up the Greenway on the left.

At the end, follow signs round the junction and continue on an alley beside the stream. Continue beside grass, to the junction (signed left for the centre) under the railway line, or go straight on beside the railway for Totterdown – make your choice.

Above: A pleasant bridleway view from Point 2. Below: Alternative transport in case you get a puncture (spotted below Dundry).

Cleeve Hill MTB

Great descents in atmospheric sub-Mendip woodlands.

The slopes of forested Cleeve Hill and its neighbours make a nice off-the-beaten-track mountain bike destination with three enjoyable descents, relatively steady climbs and sweet forest tracks. Many riders bypass its charms on their way to the Mendips proper, but Cleeve provides a satisfying, easier, less-exposed time on the bike. This route is a double loop, meeting at Brockley Combe, to grab as much legal track as possible.

Begin at the climbers' car park upside of Cleeve (also used by walkers to Goblin

Combe which is footpath-only). From there head uphill on road towards a bouncing descent to Wrington. Climb back up steadily into the woods and take a flying undulating forest track past the end of Bristol International Airport runway, to Brockley Combe. The north loop heads towards the good descent to Backwell, then climbs steadily back towards Brockley Combe. The rest of the southern loop runs along the south topside of the combe through atmospheric woodlands – where it is easy to get lost – and descends back to the A370 for a 2km warm-down to the Lord Nelson family pub.

RIDE INFORMATION

Distance	20km (12.5 miles)
Car-free	14.5km (9 miles) (72%)
Grade	Moderate off-road (several climbs and descents, nothing too steep or scary)

Suitability for children and occasional riders?
Not recommended

Traffic
There is 2km along the busy A370

Start/finish
Car park for Goblin Combe 400m southeast of Cleeve, at the turning off the A370 at the Lord Nelson pub, signed camping and caravanning

Stations
Nailsea & Backwell (1.5km off north end of route) and Yatton (4km from start/finish)

are well served from Bristol Temple Meads (Mon-Sat twice an hour, Sun once every two hours; journey time around 15 minutes. Bikes are carried free subject to space, outside rush hour)

Refreshments
The Lord Nelson pub in Cleeve (family bar meals and outside tables)

Literature
Ordnance Survey Landranger map 172

Bike shop
In Nailsea – Nailsea Cycles, 6 Clevedon Walk (tel: 01275 858000) and 132 High Street (tel: 01275 855800)

What to see
Aircraft in and out of Bristol International Airport, 500m east of route; Brockley Wood in sunshine

The start of the nice descent to Wrington.

1 From the car park head up the road for 2.2km (good views to the Mendips). Go right on the bridleway beside Oatlands Farmhouse and descend interrupted (watch out for rocky steps) to Wrington. At the roadway at the bottom by the church, go left and continue for 550m to the 'Give Way' sign in School Road.

2 Turn left, signed 'No Through Road' and go back up the hill. Continue climbing in mostly the same direction to the top. At the top continue in the the same direction for 2.2km, first with woods on your left and open land to your right (the airport approach) then in woods, as far as the road in Brockley Combe.

3 Go right up Brockley Combe, and after 250m head steeply left up the rocky

A forest track through Wrington Warren.

bridleway. At the top, after 300m, turn 90 degrees right uphill, signed public bridleway/ Avon Cycleway Link. At the first junction, continue straight ahead uphill. After another 500m, at a T-junction on a corner go left, signed Home Farm. At the drystone wall corner after 300m, turn 90 degrees right and at the road on Backwell Hill, cycle right and just before the T-junction at the end, take the bridleway on the left, opposite the white house called Pendennis. Continue straight ahead on the path between the hedges, and descend with care, watching out for pedestrians.

4 Exit left on the roadway at the bottom, on the outskirts of Backwell. At the end go right, and on reaching the quarry bear right downhill. After 200m head left into Church Lane, and continue to the main road, the A370, at West Town. Turn left and continue for 750m, then left uphill, signed for Chelvey Batch.
  After 400m, go left again, uphill on tarmac, signed Woodlands/Ambassadors Club. After 500m, fork right off the roadway on to the bridleway. Continue in the same direction, rejoining the outward route, and continuing back down to the Brockley Combe Road.

5 Now go right, downhill, and continue for 550m (past where we came in), as far as a rough clearing on the left (signed 'No Tipping'). Take the rough uphill bridleway that turns back left at an acute angle through a broken aluminium gate and traverse up the hill, with old walls on both sides.
  Stay on the clear through-trail, running parallel to the combe for 1km. After that, beyond overhanging bush cover, with a ruined wall ahead, fork right (ruins on your left) and stay with that track, which steepens downhill. (A bridleway is marked ahead at the ruins, but this is unclear). Emerge at the bottom of the Brockley Combe road, and go left to the traffic lights with the A370.
  Turn left on the A370, and continue for 2km turning left again, up Cleeve Hill Road, before the Lord Nelson pub, and return to the car park.

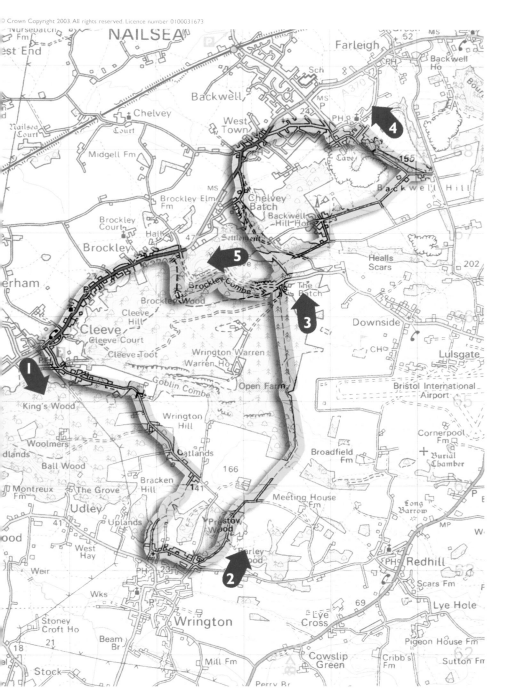

© Crown Copyright 2003. All rights reserved. Licence number 0100031673

85

Mendips MTB

You had better believe the contour lines on this excellent Cheddar-based Mendip circuit – they mean a stiff climb to a high plateau, traversing gorse moorland and long descents. Great for mountain bikers who like memories – and anyone wanting to build leg muscle.

Ten miles southwest of Bristol the limestone Mendip plateau rises up steep escarpments to 330m. An accessible, exhilarating destination for all cyclists (given good weather), the generous bridleway network around Black Down is excellent for mountain biking, with a dozen legal ladders and traverses.

Our circuit rises from visitor-friendly Cheddar to the down, and is typical of Mendip off-roading – hilly, thrilly and in wet weather, heavy going. Arm yourself with a weather forecast and an OS 182 map to explore more possibilities (see below). A short-cut (dashed) snips off 7km (and misses the pub stop at Rowberrow Bottom) to reduce a 2–3 hour riding time to around 1½–2 hours. (Don't write in if it takes you less or more time, thanks; it took the author 3½ hours with a puncture, pint of orange squash and stops for buzzards, deer and busy springtime frogs.)

The main issue is wet ground. These hills attract and hold a lot of water and all riding will be more enjoyable after a dry spell. The time you spend trudging is in direct proportion to recent rainfall and low temperatures. Vulnerable sections are the initial climb, the moorland top, entering Rowberrow Warren, and the last bridleway up to Rowberrow.

RIDE INFORMATION

Distance	24km or 17km (15 or 10.5 miles)
Car-free	17km (10.5 miles) on lanes (70%)
Grade	Moderate to difficult MTB (depending on conditions; it is one big climb)

Suitability for children and occasional riders?
Not recommended

Traffic
Light on lanes

Start/finish
Cheddar Cliff Street car park (pay & display, no height restriction)

Stations
None

Refreshments
The Swan pub (on 24km full route) has outside tables

Literature
Ordnance Survey Landranger map 182

Bike shops
None in Cheddar

What to see
Long views

Above: The Mendip plateau is worth the stiff climb up from Cheddar. Below: A flock of basking bath tubs on the top.

Warm up fast on a bridleway ascent – the biggest climb of the day – up steep pasture southeast of the town (very muddy after rain). Cross exposed high landscape on lanes, past isolated farms and dry stone walls, to the tall masts that mark the start of the moorland of Black Down (heather and gorse give it its name). Pause for the views (as far as Cardiff on a clear day) at the Beacon Batch trig point (325m) then descend due north down bumpy cropped grass. Stop before the bottom, and turn along the hill, westward towards the pub stop – the Swan at Rowberry Bottom at three-quarters distance (18km).

The final 1.6km descent is a blast (and a challenging climb another day?). Control your speed, be nice to walkers, and stop for horses.

Close all gates – we cover plenty of grazing and farm tracks – and carry a spare tube and puncture kit for likely bramble and hawthorn flats. The navigating, for a moorland mountain bike route, is mostly simple, but watch directions between the trig point and Rowberrow Bottom carefully – crosstracks are frequent. If you do go wrong, another bridleway will be along in a minute.

Other untested ride possibilities include the bridleway tight up the southern edge of Cheddar Gorge. Indeed, in wet weather, you would save a lot of muck by climbing on the road up the gorge and meeting the route on the top. Really keen riders can do the full-height northern descent, and take a break at Rickford or Langford, then make the full climb back, perhaps from the bridleway lane west of Upper Langford.

The highest point on Beacon Batch, at 325m.

goes left) and bump downhill for 1km towards Burrington Combe. When the slope lessens, at a smaller track crossroads (in line with the rock scarp to the right, east), go left, towards trees.

Continue in this direction as best you can for 2km, staying on the through-track. (The first 400m is soft and broken by rivulets, then the surface improves to a rough stone track. Ignore cross and parallel tracks as you run along the perimeter of Rowberrow Warren on the left, with some downhill.)

After 2km, the track reaches (perhaps the third) bridleway junction at a small combe (on the left, with gate). Make a 90-degree left uphill (a mire in wet weather), and climb 300m to the pink house. Go up right alongside the grounds to the tarmac lane. Turn right uphill. The Swan pub is 400m on.

1 From Cliff Street car park go right, straight ahead over the mini-roundabout, across the river, and immediately right up a little lane (the gorge road continues). Climb for 1km as far as the hamlet of Bradley Cross then, at the postbox, pivot left and take the right fork bridleway to the right of the cottage (signed).

Climb open farmland and track for 1.5km (200m height gain), staying on the best-defined route. Above Carscliff Farm, where the track begins to plateau, continue on the double-track lane for 1.5km, down to the B road.

2 At this staggered T-junction, go straight ahead on the lane (B3371 signed Compton Martin), continue for 1km to the hamlet crossroads. Turn left (to Charterhouse, NCN3) and continue for 2.9km (pass Velvet Bottom nature reserve, straight ahead to Burrington at crossroads) as far as the left turn-off towards the masts (a dead end for cars).

Climb (50m) up the bridleway to the masts. Continue on the bridleway to their left, to the moorland gate. Pace-climb (black dashed track on the map) to the trig point of Beacon Batch.

3 From the trig point, continue more or less straight ahead along the top of the moor (the track you can see for longest – a dashed black line on the map). After 750m, fork right on the bridleway, to start downhill. At a broad bridleway crosstracks, go right (a shorter route

4 (In dry conditions, you can return on the lane past the pink house and continue on bridleway up the combe for 1km to meet the route at the subterranean waterworks.)

At the pub junction, go left, uphill, and after 300m where the road bends right, keep straight ahead, on track.

Continue for 800m to houses, to the entrance bridleway on the left, for Rowberrow Warren. Take it, drop downhill to the combe, and go right (either side of the subterranean waterworks). Soon, rise left out of the combe (there is a stream on your right), at the top go right on the good forestry track, and continue to the U-bend on this track.

Go straight ahead on the bridleway through trees to Tyning's Farm & Trekking Centre.

5 Beyond the farm, go right on the tarmac lane. After 300m, where that bends right, stay straight ahead in the same direction. After 1km, the top of the final bridleway descent is reached.

On this 1.6km downhill, ride with respect for horses and walkers, and close the gates. After 1km, take the left bridleway track (but if you miss this, pick it up further on at the open slope and fencing, going down left), to emerge near the bottom on a lane, then continue 500m to a T-junction with the road in Cheddar.

Head right for 400m and after the curve round left, go left into Kent Street. Continue to the King's Head pub, go right, and left at the bottom, and back to the mini-roundabout and car park.

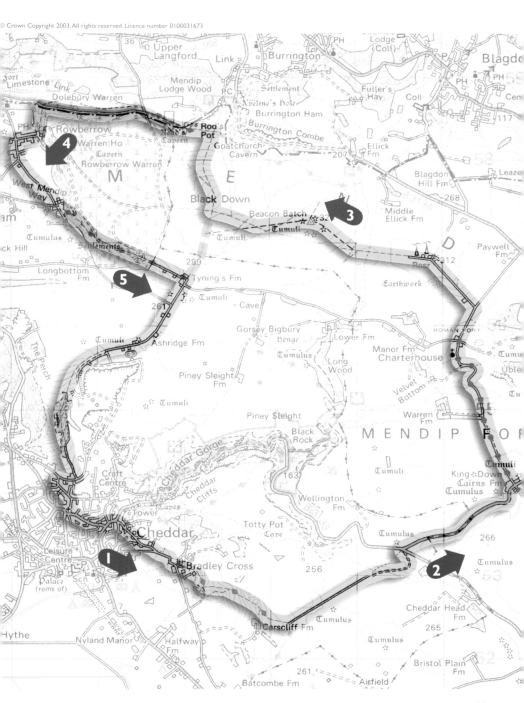

© Crown Copyright 2003. All rights reserved. Licence number 0100031673

Chew Valley lanes: Keynsham to Chew Magna

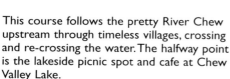

This course follows the pretty River Chew upstream through timeless villages, crossing and re-crossing the water. The halfway point is the lakeside picnic spot and cafe at Chew Valley Lake.

From bustling Keynsham (railway station) this scenic river valley ride visits the peaceful villages of Compton Dando, Woollard, Publow, Pensford and Chew Magna, each with its bridge, most with its parish church and pub. Pensford is dominated by its magnificent

disused viaduct.

Chew Valley Lake is a smashing spot on a sunny afternoon, either for a picnic or cafe snack. Thereafter comes the smart little town of Chew Magna, where you can buy provisions.

Hills rise over a rural landscape to the north, and on the elevated return leg you get high views over the landscape. Anyone wanting central Bristol can stay with the NCN3 at Whitchurch down the Railway Path (although

RIDE INFORMATION

Distance   30km (19 miles)
Grade   Moderate (it is not long, but
               has lots of rises)

Suitability for children and occasional riders?
All right for keen older children and people who fancy a scenic ride on which to get fitter, but there are narrow and fast B roads

Traffic
Several crossings over major roads requiring care; a section with traffic in Keynsham; occasional fast, narrow and steep B roads, particularly returning from Whitchurch to Keynsham

Start/finish   Keynsham railway station

Stations   Keynsham

Refreshments
The lakeside cafe at Chew Valley Lake Visitor Centre; village pubs – the Compton in Compton Dando; the George & Dragon in Pensford; a pub in Chew Magna

Literature
This partly follows NCN3 (the West Country Way) on both its long-established and developing courses into Bristol. From Whitchurch, you can stay on it down the Whitchurch Railway Path towards the city centre

Bike shops
Mountain Bikes in Keynsham (junction of Wells Road and Wellsway)

What to see
Pensford Viaduct (disused); Chew Valley Lake

Above: Beautiful rural lanes track the course of the River Chew South of Bristol.

Below: We follow the River Chew, seen here in Woollard, all the way on the outward leg.

this is quite broken, see Route 3). We close the route via Stockwood back to Keynsham.

The road rises and falls continuously, so be prepared to pedal hard, but the distance is not great, so this should suit most easy-going cyclists in search of a pleasant, but not too strenuous day out.

In Keynsham, we take a scenic route out of town, but this does involve pushing up a steep pathway and ascending a flight of stairs with the bike. Anyone who does not fancy this can stay with the traffic (see Direction 1).

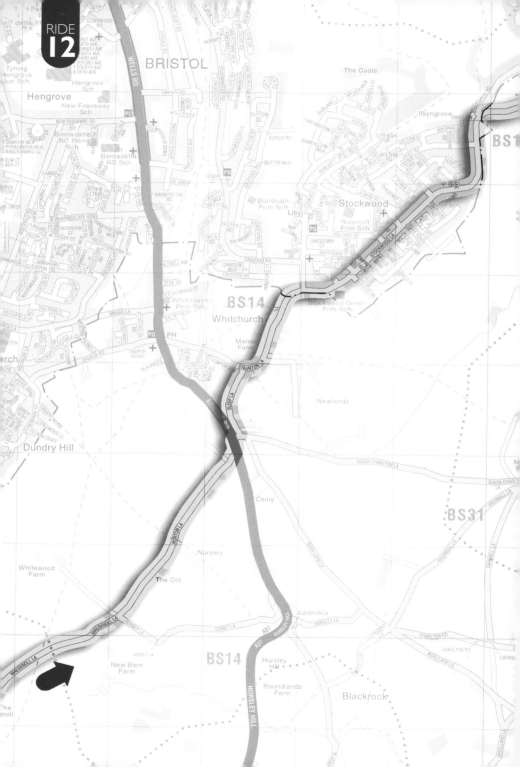

RIDE
12

BRISTOL

1 Leave Keynsham station left, on Station Road (over the by-pass). At the main junction beside the church, ride left, through the centre of Keynsham (High Street). Continue at the junction with the modern clock tower (Temple Street). After 400m, where the road bears right, go straight ahead (a dead-end for cars) down Dapps Hill. Cross over the river, and dismount to walk up the very steep path ahead, with steps at the top.

(To avoid this; at the modern clock tower junction, go left on Bath Road, cross the river and continue straight ahead on the B3116, and right to Wells.) At the B3116 road at the top, turn right.

2 After 1.2km, go right down a lane, for Compton Dando. Continue on the through-route to Chewton Keynsham and Compton Dando (pick up NCN3/Avon Cycleway). On the far side of Compton Dando head right for Woollard and Pensford. After 1km at the T-junction, go right. After Woollard, continue through Publow to Pensford.

RIDE
12

Knoll
Farm
NORTON LA
NORTON LA
Manor
Farm
CHURCH RD
Norton
Malreward
Norton
Malreward
Court
BLUE BOWL LA
Norton
Hawkfield
BRISTOL RD
Settle
Hill
Guy's
Hill
B3130
Belluton
BELLUTON
TERR
PARSONAGE
Whistley
Wood
Hammerhill
Wood
BELLUTON
LA
Traveller's
Rest
(PH)
Pensford Viaduct
PENSFORD HILL
BS39
Glebe
Farm
Byemills
Farm
Community Forest Path
Pensto
Prim Sc
Halfway
Farm
B3130
Hautville's
Quoit
PO
PENSFORD
STANTON LA
CHURCH ST
Old
Down
BS39
WICK LA
Stanton
Court
Mill
Place
Rosedale
SANDY LA
Church
Farm
PH
Preston
Farm
Stanton Drew
Prim Sch
BROOK LA
TANWELL
THE ORCHARDS
OLD CHAPEL
Upper
Stanton Drew
NEW RD
Broadoak
Farm
UPPER
STANTON
UPPER STANTON
Tyning La
Vicarage
Stanton
Drew
BROMLEY RD
Elm
Farm
STANTON WICK LA
Parsons
Farm
HIGH ST
THE CROSS
THE CRESCENT
Twinway
Farm
Carpenters
Arms
(PH)
MOORLEDGE LA
BROMLEY RD
Bromley
Farm
STANTON WICK
LA
Stanton Wick
Curls
Farm
Curls
Wood
Curl's
Farm
Utcombe
Farm
MOORLEDGE LA
Stanton Wick
Farm

3 At Pensford, cross straight over the main A37 road (towards the viaduct), then left nd immediately right (towards the viaduct ongside the church). Continue for 2km through pper Stanton Drew to Stanton Drew. At the T-nction, bear left (unsigned) and after 600m ke a little side-road, right. After 150m at a T-nction, go right and after 300m, left (neither gned) and after 1km (Gold Cross, works, rising) rn right and after 600m, just before New Town, left up Little Hollow Brook Lane.

At another unsigned T-junction, turn left, stay n the through-route and after 250m go right to hew Valley Lake and Chew Magna (NCN3 goes f to the left).

Follow the lakeside road for 1.6km. Soon after e visitor centre and cafe, go right (Denny Lane) Chew Magna.

Pretty little Pensford is dominated by the soaring disused railway viaduct.

The cafe by Chew Valley is perfect for refreshments at the turn around point.

4 In Chew Magna, turn left at the T-junction come up into the town and take the right soon after the church, at the end of the white railings (beside the 24-hour shop).

Go right (Silver Street) around the church, tur left at the church hall over the bridge and on th through-route beside the stream. At the T-junctior at the top of the lane go left and continue to Norton Hawkfield. Here, turn right to Whitchurcf At the main A37 road, go left to Whitchurch, rigf to Keynsham, and immediately left down Sleep Lane (NCN3) – with care on this narrow road.

At the mini-roundabout T-junction, head right into Staunton Lane (NCN3 goes off left), signed for Horseworld. At the mini-roundabout, Stockwood Lane, go straight ahead and continue on this road for 3km, minding the traffic and a narrow descent, all the way down to Keynsham and the main A4175.

Here, go right carefully, back to the church roundabout in Keynsham. Turn left for the railwa station.

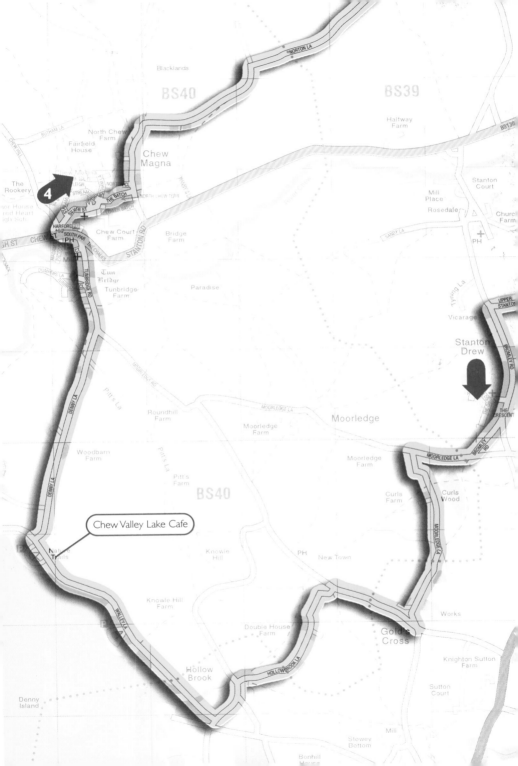

Chew Valley Lake Cafe

Bristol & Bath Railway Path

It's easy, pleasant and famous. Ride along the Bristol & Bath Railway Path and you are on a piece of the British cycling frontier. The path was one of the first cycling rail trails pioneered by engineering charity Sustrans, and formed the initial link in the chain of the expanding National Cycle Network.

The longest journey starts with the first pedalstroke!

Rich in features and being both a clear urban route and pleasant countryside amble, this railway path is unbeatable – if a little long and straight in places! It follows the trackbed of the former Midland Railway between the two cities, a line which closed to passengers in the 1960s. Cyclebag, then the Bristol cycling campaign, was responsible for initiating its construction, which took place between 1979 and 1986.

RIDE INFORMATION

Distance 26km (16.5 miles)
Car-free 24km (15 miles) (91%)
Grade Easy (surfaced throughout, and flat although gently uphill to the centre from both ends)

Suitability for children and occasional riders?
Fabulous in whole or part

Traffic
None (apart from initial side road out of Bath, Brassmill Lane, and 1km minor roads out from Bristol Temple Meads)

Start/finish
Bristol Temple Meads station/Bath Spa station; anywhere en route

Stations
Bristol Temple Meads, Lawrence Hill, Keynsham, Bath Spa

Refreshments
Kiosk at Warmley old station (weekends Easter-Sept); cafe at Bitton station (Avon Valley vintage railway), Bird in Hand pub at Saltford (outside seating and petanque), Cherry Tree pub at Oldland

Literature
Leaflet *Bristol & Bath Railway Path* from Bristol City Council and Bath & North East Somerset Council, South Gloucestershire and Avon Valley Partnership

Bike shops
Bath – Avon Valley Cyclery (tel: 01225 442442, rear of Bath Spa station), John's Bikes (tel: 01225 334633, 82 Walcot St); Bristol – Mud Dock Cycles (tel: 0117 929 2151) near the Arnolfini centre

What to see
Bitton station, home of the Avon Valley Railway, restored vintage trains steam up regularly, now extended to the Avon Valley Country Park (general enquiries tel: 0117 932 5538, 24-hour talking timetable tel: 0117 932 7296); Sculpture Trail – reflecting the character of the path. Sustrans has a leaflet with details (tel: 0117 929 0888)

Link from Bristol Temple Meads station to Railway Path

From Temple Meads, walk through the side shed (on left of forecourt) and out of the top end and to northwards cross the new square at Temple Quay (offices) to the stylish steel bridge across the harbour. Continue to the road and then follow signs up Avon Street/New Kingsley Road/Horton Street and Midland Road to pick up the start of the railway path.

Heading from the path towards the station, directions are easy in reverse to above, and the route is signed.

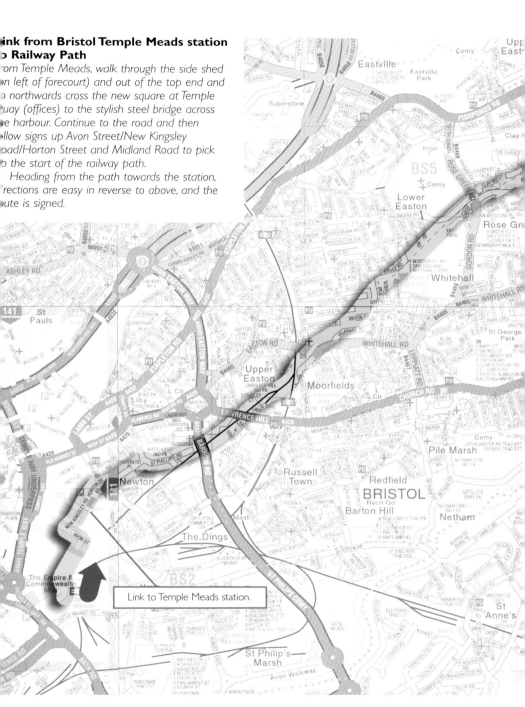

Link to Temple Meads station.

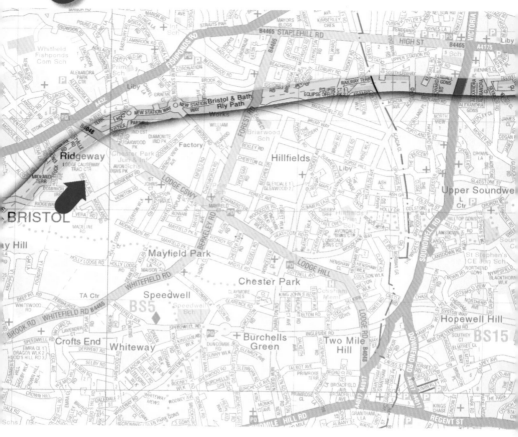

Sculptures dot the way, the 500m-long Staple Hill Tunnel in Bristol is lit and surfaced, but still bit of a thrill, there are four crossings of the rural River Avon and three nice spots to eat en route. Inhabitants of Bristol, Bath and the towns nearby won't beat it for a nice day out with the family in good weather.

You can ride directly from both main stations in Bristol and Bath, the full distance being 26km (52km return). An excellent halfway point at which to pause or turn round is Bitton station (at 15km one-way, 30km return from Bristol Temple Meads; 11km one-way, 22km return from Bath Spa). Or you can cycle from city to city and return by train (via the old GWR route).

Another feature en route, in addition to the Staple Hill Tunnel and Bitton station, is Warmley station on the outskirts of Bristol where there is a summertime cafe on the old platform.

The most scenic section is the rural stretch between Bitton and the outskirts of Bath, passing the Avon Valley Country Park (where there is a riverside picnic spot).

Sections of the path have been commandeered for other routes in this book, notably the Bristol North Explorer (4) and the River Avon & Railway Path (5).

The path forms part of the NCN4 long-distance route from Gloucester to Newbury (201km). NCN3 runs between Saltford and Bristol en route from Padstow to Bristol (405km).

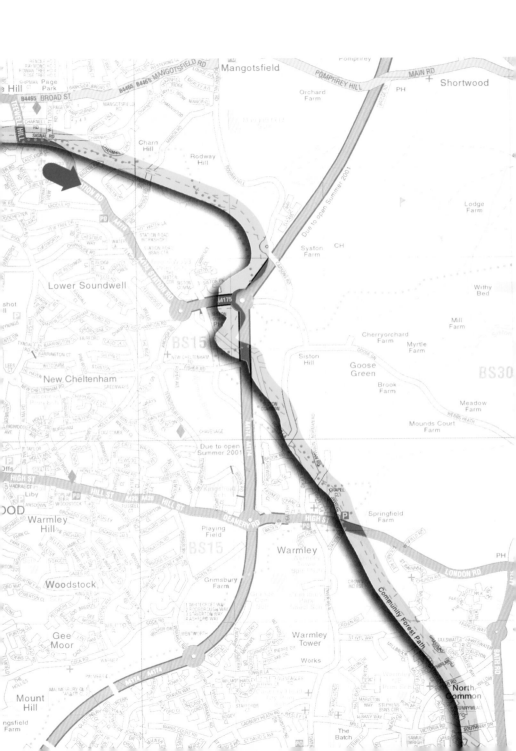

RIDE
13

Bitton Station

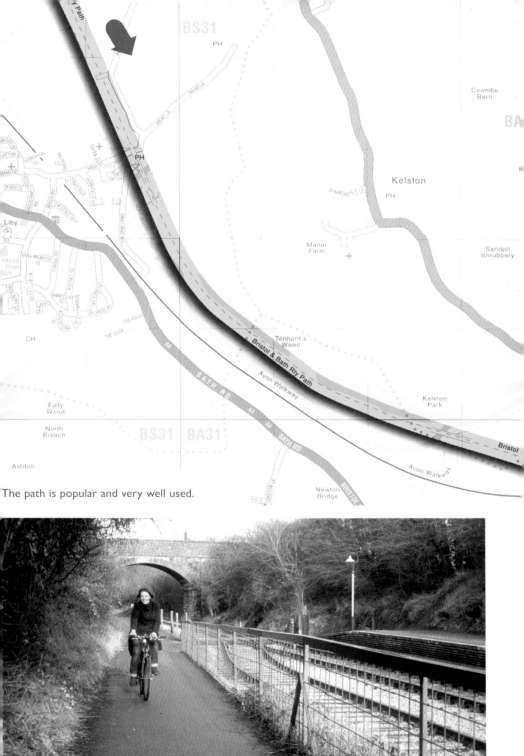

The path is popular and very well used.

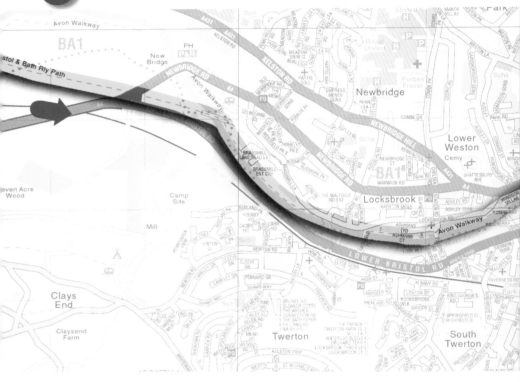

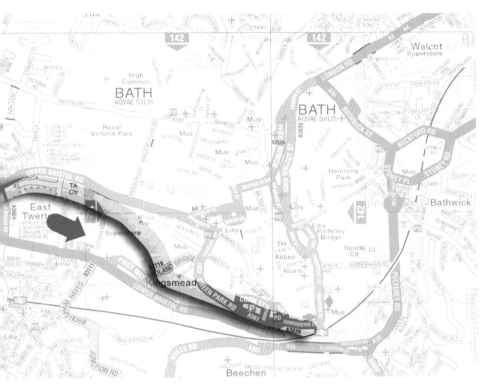

Opposite: The Avon towpath continues into the heart of Bath. Right: Riding where steam trains once puffed.

Link from Bath Spa station to Railway Path
Turn left out of the station forecourt (Dorchester Street) and continue to the junction, go left and make your way down to the Avon river towpath. Continue along the river; the NCN4 route joins from the right after 1km at Nelson Villas.

Heading towards the station: stay on the riverside path after the NCN4 has headed off left (Nelson Villas/Place, crossing through the centre of the city to the Kennet & Avon Canal) and continue 1km to the end of the path. Then meet the roadway beside the road bridge, but now walk the bike ahead round the junction left on the pavement, and stay walking right into Dorchester Street, which is the wrong way one-way in this case. The station is 200m on.

Bath Sightseeing

Enjoy Bath's delightful buildings and setting on a short route that takes in the abbey, Roman baths, beautiful terraces and a handsome stretch of canal. There is one major climb which you may avoid – but you are missing out if you do!

What to see
Bath Abbey Cathedral
Built 1499-1616 this was the last great medieval church constructed in England, and has wonderful fan vaulting in the nave. On th western façade (overlooking Abbey Churchyard) a series of angels ascend and descend ladders, as appeared to the founder Bishop Oliver King in a dream.

Roman Baths Museum & Pump Room
Built 1st-4th centuries AD, this bath complex is constructed over three natural hot springs. was restored in the 18th century when takin; the cure became fashionable and Bath becam

RIDE INFORMATION

Distance 8km (5 miles)
Car-free 1.5km (1 mile) (20%)

Grade
Easy/moderate – stiff worthwhile climb/descent to Lansdown and Camden Crescents (2.5km total)

Suitability for children and occasional riders?
Without visiting the high crescents this is suitable, although there is light traffic. Only children with good bike control should ride on the canal, although the towpath is wide and well maintained

Traffic
Mainly light but with several crossings. Watch the right turn into London Road, and the mini-roundabout to the Paragon, also going round the Sydney Place/Beckford Road roundabout towards the canal

Start/finish
Bath Spa station (or anywhere en route, eg the abbey, the Circus or the Royal Crescent)

Stations
Bath Spa

Refreshments
Numerous cafes in the city centre

Literature
Bath TIC has full information and maps on all sights; find this 100m off the south side of the abbey in Abbey Church Yard (tel: 0906 711 2000, 50p per minute; email: tourism@bathnes.gov.uk; website: www.visitbath.co.uk; open daily at least 10am-4pm).

Bike shops
Avon Valley Cyclery (tel: 01225 442442, rear of Bath Spa station), John's Bikes (tel: 01225 334633, 82 Walcot Street, below the Paragon en route)

Above: One of the nation's most desirable addresses, the gorgeous 1758 circus.

Below: Sip Bath Spa water at the Georgian Pump Room restaurant.

the town to be in. See the Roman great bath and paving, 19th-century arcading, smaller baths and the hypocaust.

The elegant 18th-century Pump Room is attached to the museum. A fountain dispenses spa water that you can sample in the uppercrust restaurant while enjoying the ambience provided by live chamber music.

The Thermae Spa is a recent revival of the functioning spa, where the Roman, medieval, Georgian and Victorian parts nearby on different sites, such as the Cross Bath and Hot Bath, have been renovated and a new modernistic spa has been added, including an open-air rooftop pool.

The Circus

This superb 30-dwelling 360-degree terrace around mature plane trees was designed in 1758 and has counted Clive of India, David Livingstone and and Thomas Gainsborough among its residents.

Assembly Rooms and Museum of Costume

The Public Room, the Ball Room, Tea Room and Card Room of the 18th-century Assembly Rooms are where Bath society gathered to

We cross Pulteney Bridge and Avon Weir en route.

Above: Cycle along the Royal Crescent as 'if you own it'. Below: However, Bath's high-level terraces, such as Camden Crescent, are just as striking, and have fabulous views.

dance, play cards and socialise. The tradition continues as folk congregate to attend wedding receptions and the like. The museum in the basement displays fine clothes from the last 400 years, including fabulously impractical ladies' crinolines. The building lies off the Circus, down Bennett Street.

The Royal Crescent
More than 1,000 rooms in this tall exquisite crescent overlook cobbles and lawns. No. 1 houses a museum that exhibits the furnishings and fittings of a fashionable Georgian townhouse of the day.

Pulteney Bridge and Great Pulteney Street
Lined both sides with little shops, this was designed by Robert Adam in 1774 to expand the town over to the east bank of the River Avon. It leads to what is judged the finest street of Georgian terraces in existence, Great Pulteney Street. At the end is the Holburne Museum of Art, with works by Turner, Stubbs and Guardi.

RIDE
14

Even the canal has Bath's hallmark Georgian elegance.

This route may be short, but with its fine features, the chances of completing it in one go are narrow. You could do one full orientation ride, and return to linger at your favourite places and views.

There is a steep climb and equal drop on the hillside up to two exquisite elevated crescents with fine views over Bath. Although you can avoid this on a shorter low route, it is recommended you make the effort – just take your time. On a safety note, the very steep descent needs good brakes and bike control. If in doubt, get off and walk down.

From the station we cruise round the abbey and courtyard beside the Roman Baths Museum & Pump Room, then pass beside the restored Cross Bath up to the first of many wonderful streetscapes: Queen's Square (you do three sides). Above that comes the Circus and a quick spur to the Assembly Rooms, while 150m west lies the breathtaking cobbled Royal Crescent, the bumpiness of the roadway a reminder of your humble transport.

This is the moment of choice between the low route and the full route which now climbs steeply for 700m up to Lansdown and

Camden Crescents. Fine streets en route sugar the pill.

We return to the centre down the main shopping street, Milsom Street, then cross Pulteney Bridge and proceed along Great Pulteney Street towards the Kennet & Avon Canal. This must be one of the prettiest pieces of canal in the country, 1.5km of ornate bridges and banks, two short tunnels, city views and a nice flight down six locks. Ride with care for yourself and others, and give way to walkers. We finish via a footbridge to the station.

1 *From Bath Spa station forecourt, walk the bike (wrong way one-way) for 80m up Manvers Street opposite, then mount and continue (with river and views, including Pulteney Weir on the right) as far as the big Victorian hotel. Go left at the High Street and round the abbey and dismount to walk left through Abbey Churchyard (Roman Baths & Pump Room). Continue under the portico and ride straight ahead down colonnaded Bath Street to Cross Bath at the end. Dismount, and walk right up St Michael's Place (past the cinema).*

Go left at the end (Westgate) and curve right up Saw Close/Barton Street (there are nice little streets on the right to explore – watch the one-way system) to Queen's Square. Ride clockwise round three sides, and continue up Gay Street to the Circus. Go round as many times as you like, and include a little diversion off at 2 o'clock along Bennett Street to the Assembly Rooms (open for viewing unless there is a function on). Leave for good at 10 o'clock (Brock Street) to the Royal Crescent, and head along that.

2 *(To stay on the shorter low route, return round the Circus and down Gay Street, go left after 150m along George Street and pick up the route after 200m right, down Milsom Street.)*

At the end of the Royal Crescent, turn right up Marlborough Buildings and at the end, dogleg right/left up Marlborough Street to St James's Square. Go up one side into St James's Park Street, and continue over the crossroads. At the top of the street, walk up the footpath to the right, and at the lawns above, stay left and

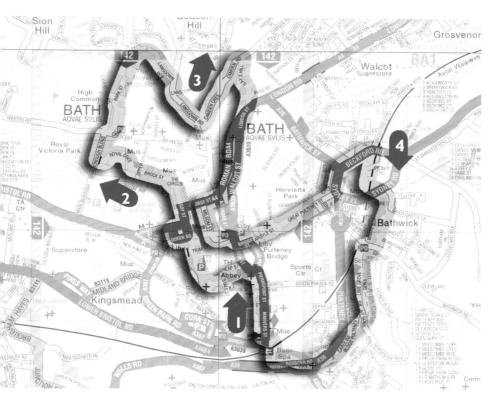

continue up to the left-hand end of Lansdown rescent.

Pass in front of the crescent to the T-junction t the end. Go carefully right downhill (Lansdown oad) and after 300m (just beside the second 1% sign) turn left up Camden Crescent.

3 Continue on Camden Crescent for 400m (becoming Camden Road) and urn sharply right – walk if preferred – down ery steep Gay's Hill/St Margaret's Hill all the ay to the bottom. At the junction with busy ondon Road, go carefully right to the mini-oundabout and straight ahead (rising) along the aragon.

At the traffic lights at the end, continue into eorge Street (in front of the Royal York Hotel) nd after 150m go left into Milsom Street. Flow und left at the end (New Bond Street), and ght in front of the Podium shopping centre

(High Street). Flow left near the abbey to cross Pulteney Bridge.

Continue straight ahead down Great Pulteney Street to the end. Go left (Sydney Place) and right carefully at the mini-roundabout into Beckford Road. After 300m, after the railway bridge, look along the canal on your left, and pick up the towpath going right beneath the bridge.

4 On the towpath, continue for 1.5km, changing sides twice, crossing Bathwick Hill road and passing several locks – give way to everybody. Emerge at the busy roadway, Pulteney Road, where the canal joins the river. Cross the road carefully and pass in front of the terrace of housing, Sussex Place. Cross the road to the riverside, and walk along the pavement to the footbridge over the river. Keep walking over the bridge and through the tunnel back to the station forecourt.

Kennet & Avon Canal:

Bath to Bradford-on-Avon

This classic route is ideal for pootlers and children. The high-grade towpath of the Kennet & Avon Canal is visually delightful and sprinkled with scenic watering holes. Set your own distance; we ride 16km from Bath Spa to Bradford-on-Avon stations – and you can also take the train out or back.

RIDE INFORMATION

Distance	16km (10 miles)
Car-free	15.5km (9 2/3 miles) (96%)
Grade	Easy-peasy

Suitability for children and occasional riders?
Absolutely perfect, with children's seats, trailers and helmets also for hire at Dundas (Brass Knocker Basin) and Bradford. The only fiddly bit is the first 1.5km of towpath from Bath Spa station, which has one staircase, climbs up six locks, crosses sides and goes through two tunnels – but it is all perfectly rideable

Start/finish
Bath Spa station/Bradford-on-Avon station

Traffic
Only the last 500m through Bradford to the station

Stations
Bath Spa, Avoncliff, Bradford-on-Avon (outside rush hour, on local trains bikes are carried free subject to space, long-distance trains £1 if booking two hours or more in advance, £3 if booking within two hours of departure; 14-minute journey time)

Literature
The route is part of the 206km Severn & Thames NCN4, full map and details available from Sustrans (tel: 0117 929 0888); Ordnance Survey Landranger maps 31/173; Kennet & Avon Canal map (£4.75, GeoProjects, tel: 0118 939 3567)

Refreshments
The George Inn at Bathampton (4km); the Viaduct Inn and Angelfish Cafe at the Waterways Visitor Centre at Brass Knocker Basin (9.5km); Cross Guns freehouse and Mad Hatter Cafe at Avoncliff Aqueduct (13.5km); the Lock Inn Cafe, Canal Tavern and Barge Inn at Bradford (15.5km)

Bike shops/hire
Dundas Canal Co. at Brass Knocker Basin/Dundas (eg £14 per day, tel: 01225 722292); Towpath Trail Bikes at the Lock Inn at Bradford (eg £12 per day, tel: 01225 868068); in Bath – Avon Valley Cyclery (no hire, tel: 01225 442442, rear of Bath Spa station) – John's Bikes (no hire, tel: 01225 334633, 82 Walcot St)

The scene at the Bradford end of the route.

What to see

Claverton Pumping Station (7km), with a waterwheel-powered beam engine pump built in 1813 by canal engineer John Rennie, that can still raise water 14.3m from the River Avon up to the canal (tel 01225 483001 for open days and pumping days); **Dundas Aqueduct** (9km), 1805, is considered Rennie's best work; the **Waterways Visitor Centre** at Brass Knocker Basin at the end of the restored ½km of the Somerset Coal Canal, where it branches off at Dundas Aqueduct (9.5km); **Avoncliff Aqueduct** is higher than Dundas and now features modern stonemasons' engravings as well as original ones (13.5km); **Bradford-on-Avon** sights (15.5km, tel: 01225 865797) include the 14th-century tithe barn, Saxon church, and medieval town bridge with chapel.

Everyone loves the Kennet & Avon Canal cyclepath between Bath and Bradford. Unless it's raining hard you won't be alone, and even

then the narrowboat folk go about their business. In summer months the path is crowded with holiday pedallers, going short or long distance, one-way or return, continuing further west on the Bristol & Bath Railway Path or eastward on the canal as far as Devizes and beyond on NCN4. Bath-to-Bradford return clocks in at only 31km, which makes a satisfying goal for the day. If you are feeling too drowsy from sun or beer, the train journey is the quick way home.

Please ride with care and consideration for others, and keep a close watch on children (read the Waterways Code, page 11). You should obtain a free canal cycle permit (British Waterways tel: 01380 722859).

From Bath Spa station we join the canal almost directly. The first 1.5km has the only rise in the route (up six locks), several romantic examples of Georgian architecture and two short tunnels. Thereafter, the landscape becomes steadily rural. Pass Bathampton (4km) and turn south into the wooded valley of the Avon river. Pass Claverton Pumping Station at 7km and impressive Dundas Aqueduct at 9km (please dismount; see What to see).

Dundas also doubles as an old canal junction, where the former Somerset Coal Canal comes in from the right, the south. The first ½km still functions as moorings, and at the end you find the contemporary Waterways Visitor Centre (with toilets), also a cafe, bike hire and pub (take the path off the south side of the aqueduct, then the low path if the canalside high path is closed). Beyond this point, the canal, which went to coalfields up the Midford Valley, is filled-in (see Route 13).

The Avoncliff Aqueduct (at 13.5km, please dismount) is elegant as well as spectacular, with outside seating at both canalside cafe and pub (and a railway station). You have to pass beneath the viaduct to stay on the towpath here. Two kilometres further, past the 14th century tithe barn, is another gathering place for summer crowds, and a neat turnaround or finishing point.

❶ *From Bath Spa station forecourt, go right and walk through the subway beneath the tracks. On foot, continue across the green footbridge. At the far side, go carefully left for 150m along the road, then drop down to the lockside towpath (where the Kennet & Avon Canal joins the River Avon).*

Go right (there is a lock on your left), under low bridges and up the steps. Cross the lockgate left to the far side of the towpath, and go right up past six locks (with the canal on the right). Continue for 1.5km (switch sides twice, through two short tunnels) to the edge of Bath.

❷ *Continue for 14km along the towpath to the edge of Bradford-on-Avon. Moving away from the towpath, continue past the tithe barn, to the end of Pound Lane. Go left carefully on main Frome Road, continue for 150m and take the station road left.*

The NCN4 continues along the canal via Trowbridge to Devizes (another 18km); go right on Frome Road, and soon left (the canal on your right).

Crown Copyright 2003. All rights reserved. Licence number 0100031673

Pumping Station

Dundas Aqueduct

Brass Knocker Basin

Avonmouth Aqueduct

115

Bath South lanes: Monkton Combe to Saltford

Tour pretty valleys and villages south of Bath, on a hilly road circuit with a low car-count

For fit cyclists, or people who want to get fit, this wonderful circuit is full of testing climbs but also a treat for the senses. On scenic lanes along the tranquil valleys of Midford and Cam Brooks you can imagine yourself a good distance from any city, in what is indeed the southern end of the Cotswolds. Villages are pretty and their pubs well spaced for a bevvy.

The route is also cycle-friendly. It opens on the car-free Kennet & Avon Canal towpath and closes on the car-free Bristol & Bath Railway Path. The lanes in between form the nub of the route and carry little local traffic.

Expect to be out of the saddle climbing at several points; from the canal to Monkton Combe, out of Midford, beyond Combe Hay, the 900m after Dunkerton (a straight ascent out of the valley), and beyond Priston.

RIDE INFORMATION

Distance   39km (24 miles)
Car-free   16km (10 miles) (42%)
Grade   Moderate-difficult
                  (depending on your fitness)

Suitability for children and occasional riders?
Not recommended

Start/finish   Bath Spa station

Stations   Bath Spa

Literature
Ordnance Survey *Landranger map 31* (for more information on Bristol & Bath Railway Path see Route 3, and the Kennet & Avon Canal Route 13)

Refreshments
The George pub at Bathampton; Angelhair Cafe at the Canal Visitor Centre

at Brass Knocker Basin; Wheelwrights Arms at Monkton Combe; Wheatsheaf at Combe Hay; Ring O' Bells in Priston; Bird in Hand at Saltford

Bike Shops
Bath – Avon Valley Cyclery (tel: 01225 442442, rear of Bath Spa station), John's Bikes (tel: 01225 334633, 82 Walcot Street, below the Paragon en route)

What to see
Claverton Pumping Station and Dundas Aqueduct (see Route 13 Kennet & Avon Canal); Canal Visitor Centre at Brass Knocker Basin (400m beyond Dundas Aqueduct); villages of Monkton Combe, Combe Hay, Dunkerton and Stanton Prior; lengths of disused Somerset Coal Canal from Brass Knocker Basin to Combe Hay, and disused railway line

The view back down to Dunkerton after the biggest climb on the ride!

RIDE
16

There are just a couple of busy traffic crossings: the A36 after Dundas Aqueduct, and the A4 at Saltford.

Nearing the end of the route, there is a short-cut back to Bath that saves 10km and avoids Saltford and most of the railway path (see dashed line).

1 *From Bath Spa station forecourt, take the subway to the right (looking from the doors) beneath the tracks, and walk over the footbridge across the River Avon.*

On the far side, go left carefully on the road and after 200m turn left down to the lock that connects the river and the Kennet & Avon Canal. Follow the towpath on the right of the lock, beneath the road bridge (two low bridges), go up the stairs and at the top, cross over the lock gates to the left bank of the canal.

Continue right along the canal towpath for 9km as far as Dundas Aqueduct (the first 1.5km is slower, uphill, crosses banks twice, the roadway once and passes through two tunnels). Thereafter things are straightforward.

2 *At Dundas Aqueduct (beside Claverton Pumping Station and the opening section of the Somerset Coal Canal), cross the bridge to leave the canal up the lane to the right (past the B&B) to the main A36 road. (The cafe at the Canal Visitor Centre at Brass Knocker Basin lies 400m along a narrow path continuing in the same direction beside the old section of Somerset Coal Canal.)*

Cross carefully directly over, and climb to a crossroads. Continue straight over to Monkton Combe, and continue on the main route through the village.

On the far side of the village, go left (to Tucking Mill and Midford). At Midford continue through the village and stay straight ahead (to Combe Hay).

In Combe Hay at the second, staggered crossroads go straight ahead (to Dunkerton), and soon left (also Dunkerton). At the A367, go carefully on the pavement right and then left, to continue in the same direction as far as Dunkerton.

© Crown Copyright 2003. All rights reserved. Licence number 0100031673

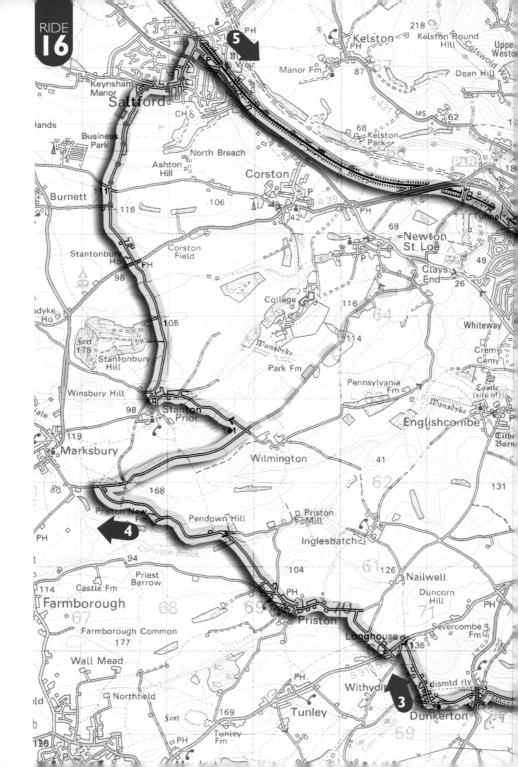

The pastoral scene at Dunkerton.

3 In Dunkerton (opposite the church on the left) go right, uphill, the biggest climb of the route (70m in 900m), to leave the valley.

At the T-junction at the top, B3115, turn left and after 150m, right to Priston. Continue through Priston, and at the junction on the far side, go right to Marksbury.

4 After 2.3km (1km before Marksbury), where the road bends 90 degrees left, turn right up the lane and continue for 1.6km up and over the hill. (After 250m, depending on conditions and your bike, you can go left on the byway which leads directly to Stanton Prior.) At a small crossroads turn left downhill into Stanton Prior.

(You can take a 10km short-cut to Bath outskirts, by continuing straight ahead here, to Clays End, the A4 and the Bristol & Bath Railway Path if desired – untested.)

On the outskirts of Stanton Prior, continue where a dead-end road leads off to the right. At the T-junction in the middle of the village go right and continue for 1.6km to the main A39. Travel carefully straight ahead, to Saltford.

Before Saltford, we join the Avon Cycleway/NCN3. On the edge of Saltford, at the T-junction turn right (Manor Road), and right again down to the main A4. Cross carefully and go straight ahead to the T-junction. Turn right and drop down to the Bird in Hand pub. On the far side of the railway bridge, ride right up the ramped pathway on to the Bristol & Bath Railway Path.

5 At the railway path, go left, slightly downhill, southeastward, and continue for 4.6km to Bath.

On approach, follow the NCN4 along the road at Brassmill Lane and on to the Avon riverside path. Continue on this obvious riverside route as far as you can (the NCN4 turns off at Nelson Villas) emerging in the centre at Park Road just before the Churchill Bridge roundabout bridge.

Dismount and walk the bike right along the pavement back to the station, first to the road bridge (Broad Quay), then curving left and right into Dorchester Street (one-way and the wrong way for us).

Bath South MTB – Wellow Valley

Save this pretty off-road tour of undulating farmland south of Bath for summertime, when the tracks are rideable and fun. Visit the long barrow at Stony Littleton, and tackle an additional stinging downhill if you really really want ...

Open skies and long verdant slopes in the second valley south of Bath form an English landscape with lots of climbing and moderate

technical challenge – unless you opt for an extra mad descent down Pipehouse Lane at the end (experienced riders only). Starter mountain bikers can choose for the shorter route.

The Wellow Brook babbles down Wellow Valley to Midford Brook en route for the River Avon near Dundas Aqueduct. Bridleways and byways abound, but they are trod by cows and horses, and only rideable in the dry.

RIDE INFORMATION

Distance
Main route 20km (12.5 miles); short route 14km (9 miles); Pipehouse Lane Loop 8km (5 miles). Full route 28km (17.5 miles)

Grade
Moderate-difficult (hilly, rutted, heavy going in wet weather)

Suitability for children and occasional riders?
Not recommended

Start/finish
Hinton Charterhouse on the B3110 (very hilly 8km south of central Bath), or Wellow

Stations   Freshford

Traffic
Mostly light in lanes, with section on Pipehouse Lane Loop on the A36

Literature
Ordnance Survey Landranger map 172, with 1.5km on map 183

Refreshments
Rose & Crown (real ale, bar meals and restaurant), and Stag Inn in Hinton Charterhouse; Faulkland Inn and store (hot food and drinks) at Faulkland; the Fox & Badger pub and store at Wellow; Hope & Anchor in Midford

Bike shops
6km north of Hinton Charterhouse, Bath & Dundas Canal Co. at Brass Knocker Basin/Dundas (eg hire £14 per day, tel: 01225 722292)

What to see
Stony Littleton long barrow (aka Wellow Long Barrow, see www.themodern antiquarian.com), a well-preserved chambered Neolithic tomb with a sheltered entrance, overlooking Wellow Brook – take a bike light, but leave the bike at the start of the short footpath; fine villages Freshford and Wellow; disused railway viaduct crossing at Midford

The rural bridleways of the Wellow Valley can be a joy in good weather — and very muddy when it's wet.

From the village of Hinton Charterhouse jump south to Norton St Philip to hit the dirt through fine farmland and make two climbs up to the southern ridge of the Wellow Valley. The main route continues round via Faulkland (and the Faulkland Arms) then descends to Wellow Brook and the hamlets of Single Hill and Stony Littleton. To visit the long barrow just beyond, please drop the bike and walk across the footpath that branches off the bridleway (do not cut across the field). Continue through Wellow and enjoy a contouring ride along the valley, then only a moderately stiff climb up the combe to pop back out at Hinton Charterhouse. And if you have the energy left, go tackle Pipehouse Lane . . .

After wet weather the tracks become unrideable, and the gate-mouths mired. Thorn punctures are likely with all the hedge trimming, so carry spare tubes and a puncture kit.

Short route

Cut out 6km near the halfway point by dropping directly through Home Covert to Stony Littleton and rejoining the route again 250m before the footpath to the long barrow.

Pipehouse Lane descent loop

From Hinton Charterhouse, a 6km anticlockwise loop takes in a wicked byway descent, Pipehouse Lane, between Park Corner and Midford. Good technical riders will find the deep-sided steeply stepped stony stream bed a challenge. Beginners – don't do it. Everyone should ride under control and at your own responsibility.

From Hinton Charterhouse, follow the yellow road northeast to the A36, turn left (north) and go 1km, then turn left at Park Corner. Stay on the through track for 1.2km, then go left, down-hill, down a track becoming stonier, as it descends.

At the road at the bottom, B3110, go right through Midford, and just beyond the viaduct left on a lane. Climb for 1km, and at the top of the hill go left, down towards scattered houses. Stay with the track, bending right and then downhill left, along the byway, beneath the disused railway. At the bottom, rejoin the main route, and ride back up to Hinton Charterhouse.

RIDE 17

Main route

1 From Hinton Charterhouse, follow the B3110 with care south for 2.1km towards Norton St Philip. Then, 200m after the width restriction on the outskirts of Norton St Philip, take the second right, Chevers Lane. Continue over the little crossroads and descend the lane to the bottom. Just beyond the left-hand bend, go of-road right, up beside Burrgate Cottage, signed 'Public Right of Way to Hassage'. Continue to the farm buildings, then cross the stream (potentially very muddy). Climb up the field on the far side, on the clear track parallel to the hedgerow.

At the brow of the hill, continue straight ahead on the gravelled track down into Hassage. In Hassage, go right (Hassage House on your right) and continue to the stream at the bottom of the hill. Kink slightly left, and continue up the field straight up the hill towards the trees, with the hedge on the right (again, potentially very muddy). At the gateway in the trees halfway up the hill, go through to the upper field, and ride clockwise left round its edge to the top side (there is a right of way straight through the field, but we go round the edge). Don't exit at the top left-hand corner, but continue to the middle of the top side, and turn left, straight across the uppermost field to the lane.

2 Turn left on the lane and continue for 1km to a cottage and road junction.

(Short route, saves 6km: go right down the byway through Home Covert, then branch right and head along the hill above Stony Littleton.)

Then, 50m on, take the bridleway signposted at a narrow angle across the field right. Keep the hut-on-a-hill on your right and stay high along the field, to drop after 200m to a gate in the wooded fence-line below.

Go through the gate, and keep to the bridleway around the edge of the fields for 1km, for as far as the double-track farm lane. Follow that left, for 300m towards Faulkland.

3 Just before emerging on the main A366 in Faulkland (where there is a pub and a store with hot food and drink), go 270 degrees right on a tarmac lane. Continue for 600m past farm buildings, to where the lane bends right downhill, and then go left on the rough track and after 10m

turn right on the signed bridleway. Follow this downhill across the field and continue for 1.8km along and down to the valley. At the T-junction at the bottom, go right on the tarmac lane into Single Hill.

4 Cross Wellow Brook in Single Hill, and climb hard 300m to the crossroads. Go right, and right again at the T-junction back across the brook at Stony Littleton. Go left 200m up the other side, on the bridleway, to Manor Farm. Continue left of the farmhouse, and through the gate across the

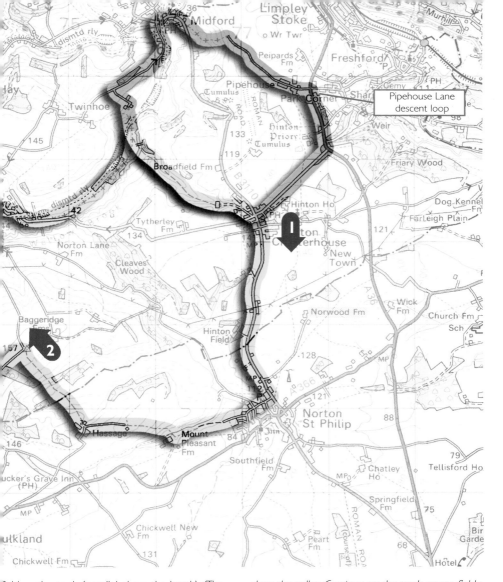

Pipehouse Lane
descent loop

field on the track (parallel above the brook). (The short route rejoins here.) Climb to the horizon gate ('the footpath to the long barrow branches left – leave the bike and walk there for viewing), and continue on the bridleway, which becomes a lane. Turn left on the lane over the ford and up into Wellow for a pub and a store.

5 At the crossroads in Wellow, go right and continue 700m. Take the byway that forks off left (signposted, before the bottom of the hill)

along the valley. Continue on the track across fields, (give way to sheep especially at lambing time) and through a gate into woods. Go through the woods, and downhill back out into the open, to the end of the field. (Pipehouse Lane Loop rejoins here.) Go right on the bridleway, and after 150m cross on the bridge to the left bank of Wellow Brook. Follow the pathway through trees to the wooden gate, and go along the main track through and up the fields for 1km as far as the houses. Continue up the lane to Hinton Charterhouse.

RIDE
18

Bath North
MTB – Lansdown

This circuit, one of strenuous, satisfying bridleways, borders the city that makes a good Sunday morning run, or local introduction to mountain biking.

The views on this downs ride are one highpoint; another is a pair of stiff low-gear climbs and equivalent rough descents. All good stuff considering the route simply turns round Lansdown on the northern edge of Bath and is easy to reach from all parts of the city. You are unlikely to be alone, and do stop for horses.

The drawback is the condition of the bridleways in wet conditions. Although surfacing has been laid on the early stretch past Kelston Hill, the hardpack becomes a

mudbath after a period of rain. Best tackle the route after a dry spell, or set out the bucket and brush at home. The route is permanently rideable by experienced riders, but not recommended for beginners whose off-road strength is still developing.

We start in the western suburb of Weston and climb hard directly for 1.5km up a lane/bridleway to the Cotswold Way passing Kelston Hill (overlooking the Avon Valley and Railway Path). Good views extend west and east to Bristol and Bath.

Descend 1.5km of double track to the village of North Stoke, and make a stiff, paced 1km climb straight back to the top of the down. Cross a golf course, then the busy

RIDE INFORMATION

Distance   14km (9 miles)
Car-free   7km (4.5 mile) (50%)
Grade   Moderate MTB (two big climbs, one rough descent)

Suitability for children and occasional riders?
Not recommended, unless they have mountain biking ambitions – it's hilly and in wet conditions very muddy

Traffic
You make your own way through Bath to get to and from the start and finish points, otherwise traffic on the route lanes is nominal

Start/finish
Start on the western edge of the city,

Deanhill Lane, at the roundabout at the end of Weston High Street; finish on the eastern edge of the city, Lambridge, where the old Gloucester Road meets the A4

Station
Bath Spa

Refreshments
None en route, lots of post-ride choice in Bath

Bike shops
Avon Valley Cyclery (tel: 01225 442442, rear of Bath Spa station), John's Bikes (tel: 01225 334633, 82 Walcot St, below the Paragon)

What to see
Long landscape views

Above: Having climbed up to Lansdown, the view west extends to Bristol and beyond.

Below: Heading for North Stoke.

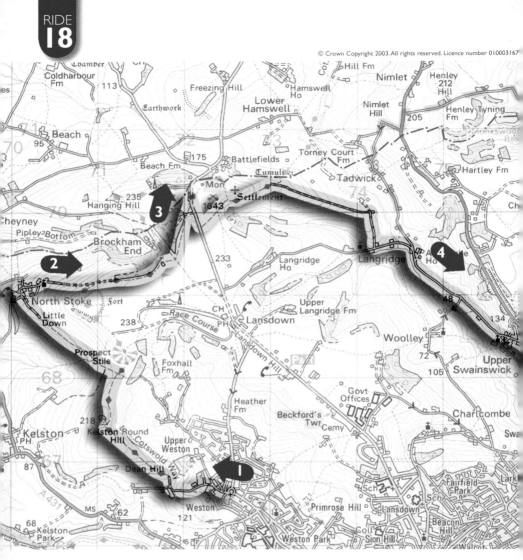

© Crown Copyright 2003. All rights reserved. Licence number 010003167

Lansdown Road for a satisfying 1.5km bridleway descent off the northeast slopes to the village of Langridge. From there we follow a pleasant lane back to the city, the old Gloucester Road, (originally the main road into Bath from the north).

You can extend the route 10km at the end, on a lovely undulating lane that runs down the next valley eastward via St Catherine (see Directions and Route 14), emerging at Batheaston a mile further east.

1 *From the roundabout at the western end of High Street, Weston, go left into Deanhill Lane. Follow the through-route up the lane, becoming off-road. Bear right at Pendean Farm (Cotswold Way bridleway), and continue past Kelston Hill (218m) to the bridleway T-junction. Go left, and descend 1.5km to North Stoke.*

2 *Stay on the lane curving round right past the church and start to climb by the green barn. Continue uphill for 1km. Continue on the*

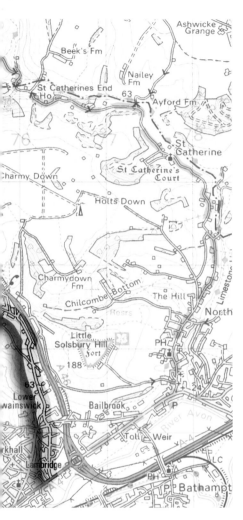

gate. Go through and continue, the route becoming a hedged double-track that descends 1km down the nose of the hill. At the buildings at the bottom (off-road ends) turn right on the lane, and at the hamlet of Langridge (a T-junction), go left.

4 At the first junction, Ashcombe House, turn right.

(A 10km scenic road route extension: at Ashcombe House go left and climb steeply via Tadwick to the A46. Go left, then carefully after 200m turn right on the lane that heads due east past Henley Tyning Farm. Continue on the lane all the way down the valley, via St Catherine to Northend. At the end of the valley near Batheaston, go right on the road parallel to the River Avon, this leads back to the A4 and Bath.)

Continue 1.9km on this lane up to the T-junction just beyond Upper Swainswick. Go right (parallel to the A46) and enjoy the easy 2km road descent to Langridge and the T-junction with the A4. Head right for the city centre.

wide track through the golf course for 600m to he buildings and wall. Continue straight ahead/right for 150m to cross tracks. Go straight ahead beside the trees for 800m, to busy Lansdown Road.

3 Go carefully right and after 350m, take the bridleway left, through the gap in the drystone wall. Cross the field diagonally, to the gate at the far corner. Stay on the track round the little rocky combe, dropping down to the

On Lansdown, approaching the start of the descent to Langridge.

Bath North lanes: Dyrham Park

A tour of lanes north of the city along the secluded St Catherine's Valley, across to Dyrham Park estate and back via Lansdown.

This circuit of hilly lanes just north of Bath has the potential to charm and to thrill. To charm in summertime when the downs are at their most blooming English – and any time of year in calm weather. To thrill with two major climbs and equivalent descents to give average-to-fit riders a workout, whether they take an hour or all day.

Making a day of it might be a good idea for easy-going riders. Not only to savour those contour lines and views, but to visit Dyrham Park (National Trust), the stately home which provides the turnaround point 13km north of the city. Cyclists can enter the park through the back gate from Dyrham village, ride to the

cycle rack (no cycling in the park) and take tea in the licensed restaurant. You do have to pay the entry fee however. Another place nearby for a bite is the Tollgate Teashop, which lies off route (see Refreshments).

From Bath Spa station we follow the towpath of the Kennet & Avon Canal for 4km as far as Bathampton, then cross the River Avon at the toll bridge (cycles free) and head up the valley of St Catherine's Brook. The first big climb of the day, 110m in 1km, leads out to the charming quiet town of Marshfield. Thereafter, cross the plateau and A46, to descend to the village of Dyrham. Lanes lead south to Doynton, then Wick.

And here is the route weakpoint: the return to the city from Wick via hilltop Lansdown. Riding 8km being buzzed by fast,

RIDE INFORMATION

Distance 36km (22.5 miles)
Car-free 3.5km (2 miles) (9%)

Grade
Moderate-difficult (depending on your fitness, there are two strenuous climbs)

Suitability for children and occasional riders?
Not recommended because of two steep up/downs, and the traffic in the last quarter

Traffic
Unfortunately, from Wick over Lansdown into Bath the traffic is often frequent and fast. Best ride outside working hours

Start/finish Bath Spa station

Stations Bath Spa

Refreshments
The George pub at Bathampton; the Tollgate Teashop lies 1.2km and a climb off-route (see Direction 3) at the 'full lane junction' turn left and climb steeply up to the A46, go right, 200m; at Dyrham Park (but you have to pay an entrance to the park and gardens; general number tel: 0117 937 2501)

Bike shops
Avon Valley Cyclery (tel: 01225 442442, rear of Bath Spa station), John's Bikes (tel: 01225 334633, 82 Walcot St, below the Paragon en route)

Above: Lanes to Dyrham. Below: Spring in Dyrham Village.

frequent traffic is hard to enjoy, despite the views. (There is little alternative without extending the distance, however. You could, for example, run from Wick southwest to Upton Cheyney and Bitton to take the Railway Path back into the centre. Or, if you have a mountain bike, there is a hilly bridleway link route from a lane that turns off east 2km after Wick, below the climb via Lower Hamswell/ Torney Court Farm and Tadwick, which brings you via Upper Swainswick back down to Bath on the pleasant Old Gloucester Road.)

Beyond Wick comes the second major climb, 130m in 1km, with an equivalent descent into Bath, 4km later. There is a flight of steps to negotiate at the start of the towpath.

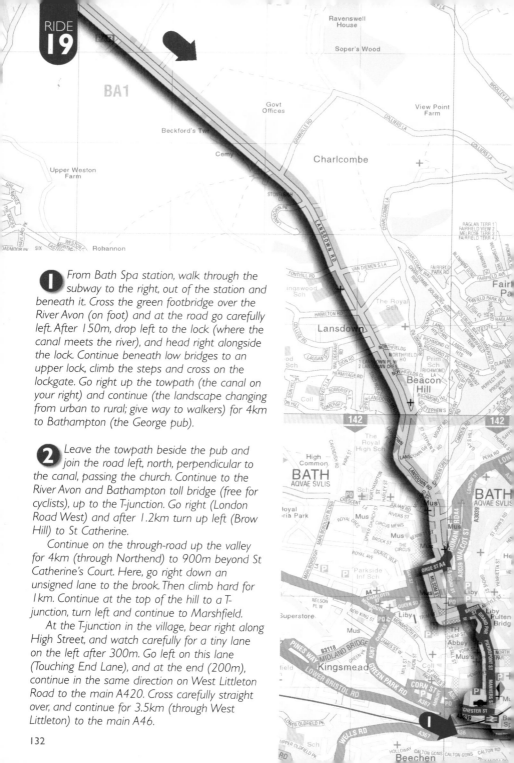

RIDE 19

**① ** From Bath Spa station, walk through the subway to the right, out of the station and beneath it. Cross the green footbridge over the River Avon (on foot) and at the road go carefully left. After 150m, drop left to the lock (where the canal meets the river), and head right alongside the lock. Continue beneath low bridges to an upper lock, climb the steps and cross on the lockgate. Go right up the towpath (the canal on your right) and continue (the landscape changing from urban to rural; give way to walkers) for 4km to Bathampton (the George pub).

**② ** Leave the towpath beside the pub and join the road left, north, perpendicular to the canal, passing the church. Continue to the River Avon and Bathampton toll bridge (free for cyclists), up to the T-junction. Go right (London Road West) and after 1.2km turn up left (Brow Hill) to St Catherine.

Continue on the through-road up the valley for 4km (through Northend) to 900m beyond St Catherine's Court. Here, go right down an unsigned lane to the brook. Then climb hard for 1km. Continue at the top of the hill to a T-junction, turn left and continue to Marshfield.

At the T-junction in the village, bear right along High Street, and watch carefully for a tiny lane on the left after 300m. Go left on this lane (Touching End Lane), and at the end (200m), continue in the same direction on West Littleton Road to the main A420. Cross carefully straight over, and continue for 3.5km (through West Littleton) to the main A46.

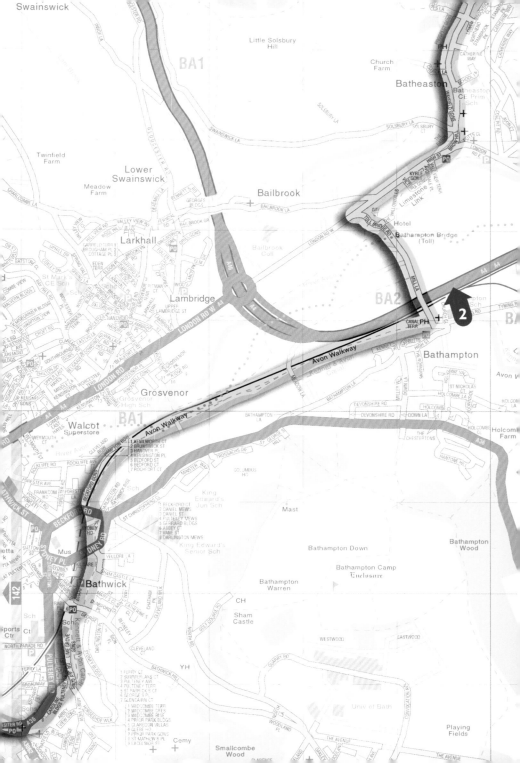

RIDE
19

Halldoor La
Poulson's
Farm

Halldoor
Wood

Ashwicke
Grange

Tipper's
Wood

Motcomb
Farm

Nailey
Farm

Ayford
Bridge

Ayford
Farm

Longley
Wood

Motcombe
Wood

Dicknick
Wood

Coombe
Wood

Court
Farm

BA1

Stillcombe
Wood

St Catherine

Limestone Link

St Catherine's
Court

Cowleaze
Wood

Lyegrove
Wood

Holts Down

Stoney La.

Ramscombe
Bottom

RAMSCOMBE LA.

The Hill

Limestone Link

Northend

**Above and below: Views of the valley of
St Catherine's**

3 Cross carefully straight over the A46 and
continue for 750m to a T-junction. Go left
and after 1km turn left again (cycle signed '17')
on a steep downhill lane. At the bottom T-junction
go left for Dyrham Park. In Dyrham village take
the first left (signed 'Cycleway') and curve round
right (ignore the church lane), past a gated view
of Dyrham Park house. (The next left leads up to
the park drive, where cyclists can ride to the
cycle rack at the house to visit and eat, but you
have to pay an entry fee; £3 in 2003.)
    Continue to a full lane junction, and right, then
after 250m, go left, head along the through-road
(through Doynton) for 4km to Wick.

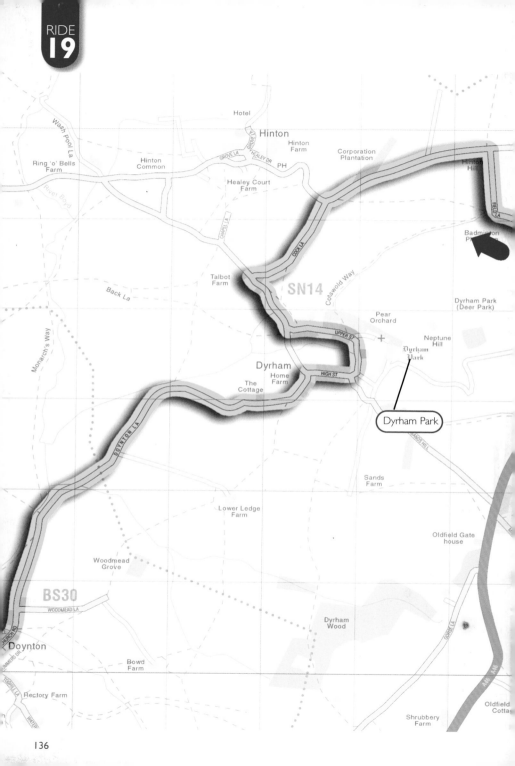

Wash Pool La

Hotel

Hinton

Hinton
Farm

GROVE LA

HEALEY DR

PH

Corporation
Plantation

Hinton
Hill

FELTS LA

Ring 'o' Bells
Farm

Hinton
Common

River Boyd

Healey Court
Farm

Badminton
Pk

CHESTL LA

Back La

Talbot
Farm

SN14

COCK LA

Cotswold Way

Dyrham Park
(Deer Park)

Monarch's Way

Pear
Orchard

Neptune
Hill

UPPER ST

Dyrham
Park

Dyrham

Home
Farm

HIGH ST

The
Cottage

Dyrham Park

DOYNTON LA

SANDS HILL

Sands
Farm

Lower Ledge
Farm

Oldfield Gate
house

Woodmead
Grove

BS30

WOODMEAD LA

Dyrham
Wood

GOOSE LA

AVE

AVE

Doynton

Bowd
Farm

Oldfield
Cottage

Rectory Farm

WATER

Shrubbery
Farm

Top: Dyrham Park, a fine stately home near the [tu]rnaround point. Bottom: And Dyrham village.

4 At Wick, cross straight over the main A420 carefully, and continue for 8km into Bath. [A]fter 2km comes a 130m in 1km climb on a [ro]ad with fast, frequent traffic.

Stay on Lansdown for a further 6km into Bath [ci]ty centre. Ride with care down the long [d]eepening descent on the Bath outskirts. Go [ri]ght at the junction beside the church downhill [(:]8), Richmond Road, and continue with care as [fa]r as the traffic lights junction with George [St]reet/Roman Road.

Now for 2km micro-navigating through the city [c]entre to return to the station. Go right, in front of [Yo]rk Buildings, and first left down Milsom Street [(s]hops), curve left at the bottom and go right at [th]e lights (opposite the Podium) into Northgate [St]reet. Turn left into Bridge Street, but right before [th]e bridge beside the river, Grand Parade. Shortly [b]ear left to continue in the same direction on [Pi]errepont Street/Manvers Street to the station.

Bath to Chippenham

via Castle Combe on lanes

Visit England's prettiest village on a short, hilly ride from Bath into Wiltshire, and return by train.

This town-to-town route on country lanes will be thoroughly enjoyable in the summer months, for cycling is the best way to savour English byways and villages at their finest. After a stop at any or all of four village pubs, complete the day by letting the train make the 15-minute journey back (check bike booking details, see above).

After Thickwood, we descend poetic lanes to the valley of By Brook and the lovely brookside hamlets of Slaughterford, Ford and the prettiest, Castle Combe. Ford, Castle Combe and the almost equally delightful village of Biddestone have fine country pubs.

The trip would be good for all-comers, were it not for the 150m climb in 2km that comes after Bath up to Banner Down. Most people nevertheless, can manage even that, given pauses for breath – there's a long time to recover afterwards. But other shallower, shorter hills do come later.

Starting from Bath Spa station you can take the city-centre road route out, or, if your bike is sturdy, follow the towpath of the Kennet & Avon Canal as far as the George Inn at

RIDE INFORMATION

Distance 32km (20 miles)
Grade Moderate-difficult (not long but several steep hills)

Suitability for children and occasional riders?
Not recommended – see Grade

Start/finish
Bath Spa station/Chippenham station

Stations Bath Spa, Chippenham; trains run approximately every 20 minutes; journey time 15 minutes. Advanced reservations £1 on all trains – without a reservation it is £3 and subject to space. tel: 08457 000125

Traffic
Mostly light in lanes, but busy on the A420 at Ford, and at either end in Bath and Chippenham

Literature
Ordnance Survey Landranger maps 172 and 173

Refreshments
The White Hart Inn in Slaughterford; White Hart at Castle Combe; White Horse Inn and Biddestone Arms at Biddestone

What to see
Castle Combe, the beautiful village that was a centre of wool trading and still features an arched bridge and the 13th century cross

bove: Castle Combe is one of the prettiest
llages in England.

Below: The stone-built White Hart at Ford.

athampton, and up to Northend, as detailed
Route 14.

If you fancy a quick jaunt to Chippenham,
here are short-cuts from both Slaughterford
nd Ford (the White Hart Inn) that cut off

around 6km but miss out Castle Combe – see
Directions. However, no route avoids all the
hills. The traffic is infrequent, although
occasionally fast. The most you encounter is in
Bath and Chippenham.

RIDE
20

1 From Bath Spa station forecourt, walk straight ahead down Manvers Street, one-way in the opposite direction, for 80m, then mount at the bus station (the road becomes two-way) and continue, as far as the abbey church (before the old Victorian Hotel, the Empire). Follow the road left and right around beside the abbey church (one-way), getting on the right-hand side of the road. Soon you must go right, and cross Pulteney Bridge. At Laura Place Circus, go left down Henrietta Street, becoming Henrietta Road, and continue to the T-junction with the main A36 Bathwick Street (Rochford Place). Turn left, back over the river (Cleveland Bridge) and continue to the traffic lights. Go right, signed to Chippenham, on to the A4 London Road. Continue for 2km to the big out-of-town roundabout (junction with the A46).

2 At the roundabout, go carefully straight over, signed for Northend, and continue 1.6km. In the village, go left, rising, signed to Northend and St Catherine. Continue for 1km, past the church and pub, to the right-hand turn on to clearly-signed Steway Lane. After a short drop to St Catherine's Brook, prepare for a major

© Crown Copyright 2003. All rights reserved. Licence number 01000316

140

mb, 150m in 2km, all the way to the T-junction
the top, Bannerdown Road.

Go left, and after 1.4km bend right with the
ad beside the airfield (where the minor road
ntinues straight ahead – Roman Fosse Way).
ontinue for 3.7km, to the signed turn-off right
Thickwood.

3 Turn right at Thickwood Lane, and continue
through the village and at the crossroads
raight on, signed for Slaughterford. Ride a 1km
ownhill, on a deteriorating but rideable lane, to
e bottom, the bridge over By Brook at
aughterford. Head left on the far side of the
idge, through the village, then, as you rise
irving right out of the village, take the little lane
at turns left (beside the footpath). (A short-cut
to Chippenham, misses out Ford, the White
art and Castle Combe); don't go left, but
ontinue eastward – see map.

At the T-junction, turn left across the river into
rd village. (For short-cut B to Chippenham, missing
ut Castle Combe, go right at the T-junction, do not
oss the river.) In Ford, turn right and right again
refully on the main A420. After 150m, go left,
gned for Castle Combe, and continue to the village.

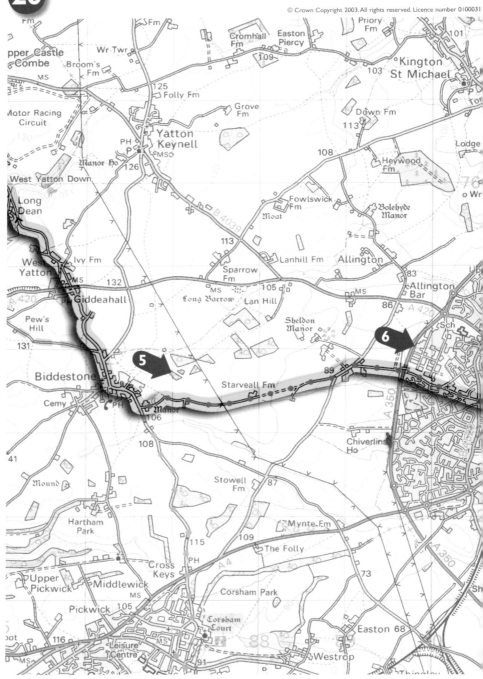

© Crown Copyright 2003. All rights reserved. Licence number 0100031

4 *In Castle Combe, continue to the medieval cross, and bear right up the hill. Continue for 800m to the B4039 T-junction. Go right, and after 400m, where the B-road swings left, continue on a minor road straight ahead, beside the motor racing circuit. Ride 1km beyond the turn-off for Long Dean, continue at the walled junction, on the main through-route straight ahead, signed to Biddestone, to the main A420 road. Cross carefully, walk the bike over the verge, and continue in the same direction beside the Crown Inn, to Biddestone village.*

5 *In Biddestone, join the through road going right, signed for Corsham, continue through the village past the green. 400m out of the far side of the village, go left to join NCN4 (past the manor house) Chippenham Lane. (Follow signs now into Chippenham centre.) Continue for 2.5km, bear left and right (this road is closed to cars) and continue to the end.*

6 *Take the footbridge over the dual carriageway, and continue in the same direction down the road, Frogwell, on the far side, in Chippenham suburbs. At the staggered mini-roundabouts, continue in the same direction, Sheldon Road. Continue beneath the railway bridge, to the T-junction with the main A4. Follow NCN4 signs left/ahead avoiding the roundabout, continuing 500m to the town bridge (pedestrianised town centre over the river to the right). Go left towards the railway viaduct. Turn right at the little roundabout in front of this and the station is at the top of the road.*

The bridge at Slaughterford is another beauty spot.

ACKNOWLEDGEMENTS

With thanks to the following for their help:

Bristol Tourist Office
Bath Tourist Office
Neil Stacey, Sustrans area manager
For British Waterways, Kennet & Avon Canal: Chris Leggett
For Bristol City Council: John Roy, John Lucas and John Richfield
For Bath City Council: Alison Sherwin
For South Gloucestershire Council: Mark Parry
For Bath & North East Somerset Council: Paul Paton
Chipps Chippendale

For support: Phil Elms, Judith Foster and Sarah Crowther and Liz Harris

Author	**Nicky Crowther**
Project Manager	**Louise McIntyre**
Editor	**Peter Nicholson**
Design	**Simon Larkin**
Page Layout	**Chris Fayers**
	James Robertson
Photography	**Nicky Crowther**

Mapping reproduced from Philip's Bristol & Bath Street Atlas © Philip's 2003 Cartography by Philip's This product includes mapping data licensed from Ordnance Survey ® with the permission of the Controller of Her Majesty's Stationary Office. © Crown copyright 2003. All rights reserved. Licence number 100011710.

Ordnance Survey maps supplied by Emapsite.com. © Crown Copyright 2003. All rights reserved. Licence number 0100031673.